Country Quilts

TIME-LIFE BOOKS

Alexandria, Virginia

Country Quilts

*styles, patterns,
and techniques from
past to present*

A REBUS BOOK

CONTENTS

Quilting Projects

General Directions · Quilting Frames
Wild Goose Chase Table Runner · Amish Star Pillows
Little Schoolhouse Quilt · Vase of Tulips Quilt

142

The American enthusiasm for quiltmaking in the 19th and early 20th centuries has left us with a legacy of quilts remarkable not only for their variety, beauty, and workmanship, but also for their importance as historical records. While the art itself did not originate here—quilting had, in fact, existed for many centuries before the first European settlers arrived—it was American needleworkers who elevated quiltmaking to an unprecedented level of social and artistic expression, creating textiles unlike any others in the world.

No 17th-century American quilts exist today, but as is clear from the few surviving 18th-century examples, the colonists borrowed from an established European needlework tradition. Already familiar with appliqué, piecing, and embroidery—the techniques that were to become the mainstays of American quilt design—early American needleworkers also brought piecing patterns, such as the Irish Chain, from their homelands. Many of these patterns are still favorites in this country.

As American quilting evolved, however, old traditions were reshaped by new circumstances. Because thread was scarce, colonial women quilted their bedcovers with a running stitch rather than with the customary English-style backstitch, which required twice the amount of thread. And as families moved West away from supplies of imported wools and linens—the necessity of using fabric scraps increased. The first "patchwork" quilts made with scraps were indeed "make-do" attempts. But by the early decades of the 19th century, thrifty yet clever needleworkers had learned how to piece scraps into the masterfully complex designs that make American quilts unique.

By the 1830s, changes in design and technique began to be affected by what women had available to them, rather than by what they lacked. Cotton had become affordable and widely accessible, which enabled needleworkers to plan their quilts, using carefully chosen colors and prints. It was at this time, as well, that the block style of quilting—a uniquely American technique in which the quilt top is made up of individually pieced or appliquéd squares—originated. Because the squares were small, it was easy for newspapers and magazines to print patterns for them, and new quilt designs spread rapidly across the country.

Perhaps the most remarkable aspect of American quilting, however, was the fact that virtually any woman could, and often did, make a quilt. Some 19th-century quiltmakers are well known: Achsah Goodwin Wilkins, for example, designed Baltimore album quilts by custom order; Susan McCord, an Indiana quiltmaker, is remembered for her garden patterns and unusual abstract works. But most quiltmakers were anonymous, stitching their memories, opinions, and dreams into fabric, yet leaving their names unrecorded. For the most part, quiltmakers regarded themselves as homemakers, not artists, and it is the unpretentious quality of their work that is so appealing today.

A Gallery of Quilts

a close-up view of an American art form

Whether they lived in a busy eastern city or were settled on the frontier, the thrifty needleworkers who made quilted bedcovers in this country produced something finer than practical spreads: the works they stitched were often highly decorative and exceptionally well crafted. What started as a simple household task became an original and complex art form.

While the possibilities for quilt patterns were—and are—infinite, the basic structure of quilts has remained standard. In general, a quilt has three layers: a backing, a middle layer of batting, and a decorative top. It is the actual "quilting"—the designs formed by tiny stitches—that usually holds the layers together.

This chapter will acquaint you with a wide range of quilt types, from wholecloth bedcovers to intricate crazy quilts. It will also show how the varied techniques for making and embellishing quilts—piecing, appliqué, stuffedwork, embroidery—have been used separately and together to create the distinctive look that defines American quilts today.

A corner detail shows the intricacies of a pieced-and-appliquéd Star of Bethlehem quilt.

Early Wool Quilts

Wholecloth quilts, like the early-19th-century worsted example above, are often called linsey-woolseys today. This name actually refers to a type of fabric that originated in Linsey, England.

The first quilts known to have been made in America were not the cotton patchworks familiar to most people today, but solid-color, quilted wool spreads. Heavy and warm, wool quilts were common—especially in the Northeast—from about 1730 to 1830.

Today, such quilts are frequently called linsey-woolseys, although the term is not literally correct. Linsey-woolsey was actually a fabric made of linen or cotton woven with wool, and in colonial times, it was typically used for clothing rather than bedding.

Early wool quilts were more often made from imported English worsteds: two or three, and sometimes more, lengths were joined to make a "wholecloth" large enough to cover a bed. Especially favored were glazed worsteds, such as calamanco, which had lustrous finishes.

Made of calamanco, the quilted wool spread above was designed for a four-poster bed. Wool quilts were often interlined with unwashed wool fleece. The natural oils helped keep moths away.

Heirloom Whitework

The tree of life in the center of the 1796 whitework quilt at right is similar to motifs found on printed Indian cottons fashionable at the time. Such fancy quilts were often finished with a fringed border.

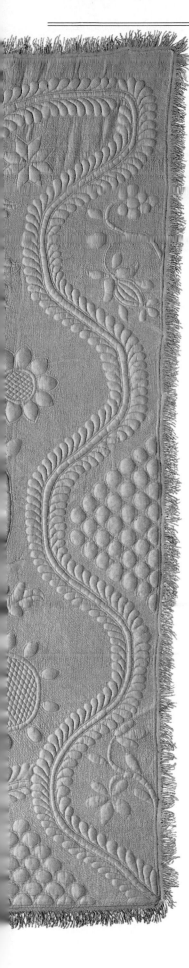

Made with fine white cotton or linen tops and elaborate patterns stitched in white thread, the whitework quilts produced between 1790 and 1830 are thought by many to be the high point of American quilting. Extremely elegant, these quilts were not designed for warmth—they often had no batting at all—but were conceived instead as heirlooms. One quilt could take from six months to two years to complete, with some quilting designs requiring as many as a million delicate stitches.

Infinite patience was also needed to produce the "stuffedwork" designs that were a popular technique for whitework. After the quilting was completed, the weave of the backing—a coarser fabric than the quilt top—was separated with a needle to make a tiny hole in each motif. Wool stuffing—and candlewicking for the stems and vines—was pushed between the quilt layers to add dimension to each motif, and the weave was maneuvered back into place. Once the quilt was washed, no trace of the holes remained.

A central medallion like that stitched on the quilt above was a common design for whitework. The background areas, which appear smooth, are actually closely spaced stipple, or dotlike, quilting.

Pictorial Appliqué

Forks Town Ship Sullivan county September 28 · 1855 Pa

The colors and heart-shaped motifs of the appliqué quilt at right are typical of those used in 19th-century Pennsylvania quilts. The actual design—a tree of life interpreted as a sunflower— is, however, unique.

By the early 1800s, appliqué had become one of the most popular methods for quiltmaking. The term, from the French verb *appliquer,* means "to place" or "to fasten on": in appliqué quilts, dozens of cut-out shapes are sewn onto a plain background fabric that serves as a "canvas" for an elaborate composition in cloth. Many appliqué designs are pictorial, as opposed to abstract, with flowers being a particularly popular subject.

Appliqué is an exacting and time-consuming technique. To ensure that a repeated motif is consistent, a template is often used for tracing the motif onto the fabric before cutting. Each piece of fabric must be carefully cut to size, allowing for an even margin around the edge, which is turned under and pressed. After being basted onto the quilt top, the pieces are sewn down with "invisible hemming" or decorative stitches. Usually, the entire work is then quilted.

Narrow pieces of fabric are the hardest to appliqué because turning under the edges can be tricky. The graceful stems and vines on the quilt opposite indicate that the maker was a master of the art.

Two Styles
of Appliqué

The 1850s appliqué quilt above displays a stylized central medallion. The hearts and other personal motifs suggest it might have been made as a wedding quilt.

Two distinct styles of appliqué quilts emerged in the 19th century. In one, the fabric pieces were arranged on a wholecloth top for a single, overall design. In the other, individually designed "blocks" were sewn together to make the top.

Following an English tradition, wholecloth appliqué quilts were often made with a central medallion pattern that resembled a formal garden plan. These quilts featured an elaborate circle in the center, an outer border of vines and leaves, and small floral motifs in between. As time went on, American quilters developed variations on this design: the central medallion might be a diamond or a square, and the border could incorporate swags and bows instead of

vines. The essential arrangement of elements, however, never changed.

By the 1840s, the block method of appliqué—a purely American creation—was far more popular than the wholecloth style, and was so prevalent that it is now considered the hallmark of American quilting. Because each block was only about twelve inches square, a quilter could carry her work around. And because the patterns were small, they were easy to trace; their size also allowed them to be published in magazines. Moreover, it was much simpler for a quilter to use blocks to make a pleasing overall pattern than to devise a single large-scale design. Even so, many block-appliqué quilts show the same ingenuity as those with a single design.

The maker of the appliqué quilt above alternated Rose Wreath pattern blocks with stuffedwork blocks. The border displays the Kentucky Flowerpot pattern.

Made in Baltimore around 1840, the example of broderie perse *above is finely quilted. The original pencil marks outlining the patterns are still visible, indicating that the quilt has never been washed.*

Broderie Perse Quilts

Owned by a relative of Martha Washington, the quilt at left was made in the second quarter of the 19th century; the chintz used for the appliqué, however, dates from the 1780s. The quilting, like that on most broderie perse *quilts, is of the finest quality.*

A mong the rarest types of early American quilts found today are those known as *broderie perse*. Made between 1790 and 1850, these quilts featured chintz appliqué. Although the French term *broderie perse* translates as "Persian embroidery," such quilts were in fact only occasionally embroidered.

During the 18th century, printed and glazed cottons imported from India, France, and England were extremely fashionable in America—but also extremely expensive. When used for quilts, the colorful printed motifs and borders on these fabrics were often cut out and arranged on a quilt top to make the most of the yardage. Once America began producing its own printed fabrics in the late 18th century, designs were created expressly for use in *broderie perse*.

Most *broderie perse* quilts were produced in affluent areas in the South and East. Their extravagant workmanship suggests that their makers had not only the means to obtain costly fabrics but also the leisure time to spend on decorative needlework. Such quilts were reserved for special occasions rather than used daily; those that exist today are generally found in remarkably fine condition.

The Pieced Quilt

Each block in the mid-19th-century quilt at right displays the same Friendship Ring pattern. The design looks deceptively simple, but since every piece used in making the blocks is curved, only a highly skilled quiltmaker could have pieced these shapes together with such consistency.

The earliest known pieced quilts in this country date from the 1750s, and this type of quilt—made by sewing hundreds of small cut-out fabric pieces edge to edge—has been popular ever since. To make the pieces easy to join, they are usually cut into simple straight-edged shapes, such as squares or triangles. A skillful quilter, however, can display her talents in a pieced quilt by devising a pattern that calls for rounded or sharply angled pieces, which are difficult to stitch together into exact patterns. One such pattern popular in America is the Star of Bethlehem, which features a central star made up completely of diamond shapes.

Quilters could achieve astonishingly different effects with block patterns made from the same basic pieces by varying the color combinations or rearranging the placement of the shapes. The precision with which the blocks were designed and put together often produced geometric patterns of dazzling complexity.

Although some pieced quilts—such as the Sunburst above—were conceived as a single, overall design, most were made up of individually pieced blocks, as in the quilt at left. Sometimes the blocks simply were stitched directly to one another; or they might be alternated with solid-color squares, or bordered with sashes.

The Sunburst crib quilt above is pieced entirely from diamonds. The concentric rings of dark and light colors combined with the angled shapes give the "sun" its radiant effect.

Pieced from Scraps

The fabric scraps used in the quilt above were chosen with careful attention to color. The dark and light squares make a lively overall pattern, and the red borders provide dimension.

Although piecing a quilt is a simple craft, American women turned it into an art form through their ingenious combinations of fabric. Often, the most beautiful quilts were those put together entirely from scraps. Generally it was limited resources that compelled women to use remnants for their quilts. But even after they had the means to buy yard goods, quiltmakers continued what we now regard as a pioneer tradition by salvaging fabric.

Nineteenth-century textile factories even catered to this practice by selling bundles of remnants: it is not uncommon, for instance, to find quilts made entirely from factory samples of men's shirting. More typically, scraps were saved from home sewing projects, and as a result, many quilts now stand as an unwitting record of a family's changing wardrobe.

The scraps in the Darling Minnows quilt top, above, were saved over many years. The calicoes in the border are from the 1820s; the other prints date closer to 1840, when the top was made.

Controlled Patterns

Not all pieced quilts were made from scraps. By using store-bought fabrics chosen specifically for a certain pattern, a quilter could have complete control over the color and shading in her design—often with sophisticated results.

The quilt above is a variation on the well-known Amish Sunshine and Shadow pattern. Although the color placement at first seems ran-dom, it has been carefully worked out. The yellow squares are repeated at specific intervals throughout the quilt to create a shimmering effect much like sunlight reflecting off water.

In the Stairway to Heaven quilt opposite, each hexagon is pieced in three shades of one color for a striking optical illusion: the individual "blocks" appear three dimensional, and the diagonal rows seem to advance as well as recede.

The success of the optical tricks in the 1930s Amish quilt design above—based on a 19th-century
Tumbling Blocks pattern—is the result of choosing and placing the colors with exceptional care.

Pieced and Appliquéd

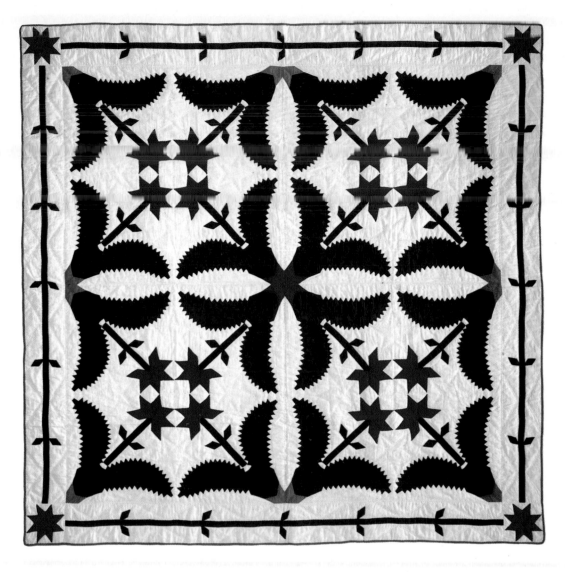

The maker of the quilt at left achieved an abstract look with geometrically stylized flowers. The red and yellow sections are pieced, the blue areas are appliquéd.

I n the early 1800s, American quilt designs were still firmly rooted in English needlework traditions. By mid-century, however, women were consciously striving to create new patterns that were also personal statements, and a recognizable American style of quilt design emerged. Many patterns began to lose their fussiness, and simplified designs intended to show off a needleworker's skillful quilting became favored.

During this period, a healthy competition developed among women who quilted. Often,

state and local fairs held contests: the top prizes went to the entrants whose pieces exhibited not only the best needlework, but also the most original designs.

One way a woman could display her capabilities in both of these areas was by using appliqué and piecing in the same quilt top. The combination allowed her to explore a variety of stitches and also expanded her design possibilities: a seemingly endless number of unique patterns could be created when pieced geometrics were mixed with appliquéd pictorials.

The unusual pattern of the Pennsylvania quilt opposite may be one of a kind. The geometric pinwheel blocks are pieced, and the orange-and-brown leaf blocks are appliquéd.

An Artful Mix

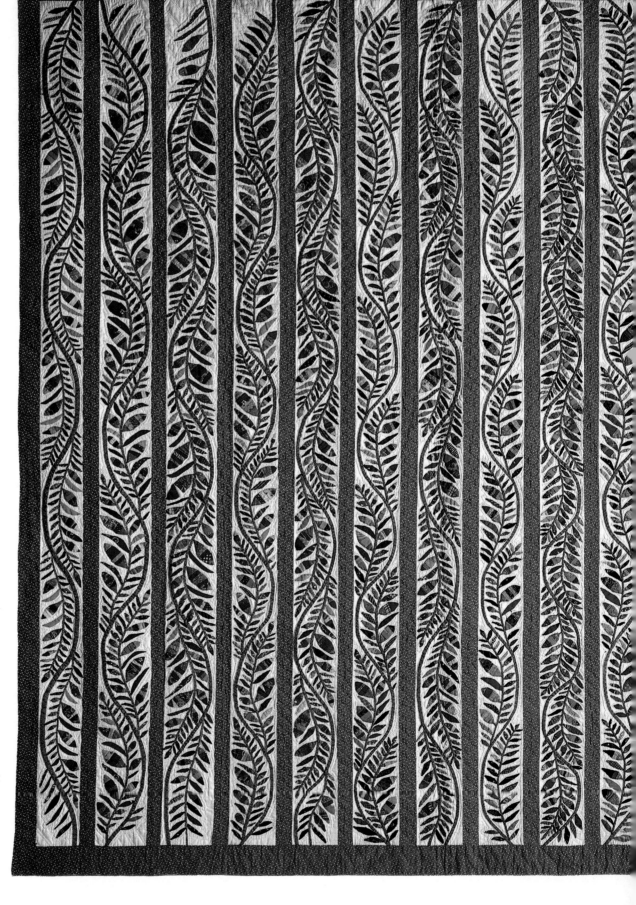

The quilt at right was made around 1845 by Susan McCord, a well-known Indiana quilter. The beauty of the design is found not only in the graceful arrangement of the vines but also in the subtle colors of the pieced leaves.

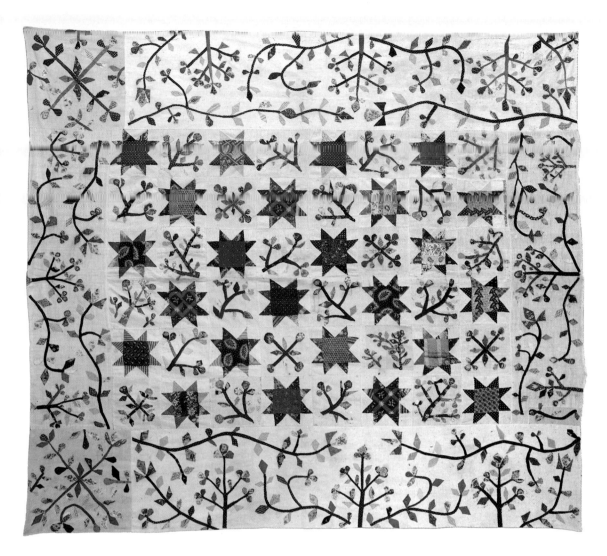

For all the pieced-and-appliquéd quilts that can be identified by a particular pattern, design, or place of origin, there are still those that simply defy classification.

Such one-of-a-kind quilts were produced throughout this country. In some cases, they may have been made by women who were familiar with traditional quilt designs but had little access to up-to-date patterns and consequently devised their own variations on favorite themes. In other instances, these quilts were sewn by quiltmakers who had a sure sense of their own artistic vision and deliberately used fabrics to create individual designs, much as a painter would use pigments.

The pieced-and-appliquéd quilt above shares some characteristics—such as the leafy border—with other quilts, but the combination of appliquéd sprigs and pieced stars in the center is unique. Moreover, all of the appliqués appear to have been cut freehand, rather than traced, giving the quilt a playful quality.

The leaves in the quilt at left were pieced together from several bits of fabric and then appliquéd. The combination of graceful vines and randomly sized leaves creates an unusually rhythmic design.

Much of the charm of the quilt above comes from the fact that none of the branches match. The airy feeling of the appliquéd sprigs intentionally contrasts with the more solid look of the pieced stars.

By using a single color combined with white, a quilter could enhance the graphic effect of geometric patterns, as in the red-and-white Sawtooth quilt above.

In the second half of the 19th century a vogue developed for pieced quilts with designs worked in white and a single color: blue-and-white and red-and-white were favorite combinations. These simplified color schemes were well suited to geometric patterns, giving them a fresh look.

It is possible that the popularity of jacquard coverlets—which were often woven in two-color patterns—may have prompted a taste for similarly colored quilts. Another theory links some of the quilts to the Temperance Movement, which used blue and white as its colors. Because blue-and-white quilts were frequently made in the Drunkard's Path pattern, they are often called Temperance Quilts.

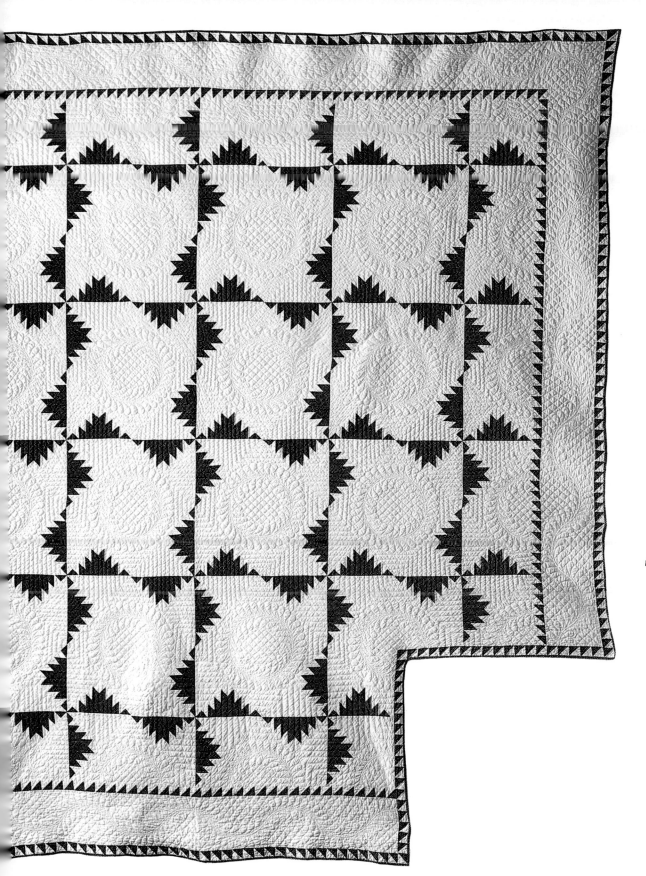

Two-Color Pieced Quilts

In many two-color quilts, the white areas display fine stitchery. The Kansas Troubles quilt at left is decorated with two traditional quilting designs: Feathered Vine along the border and Feathered Wreath in each square.

The embroidered linen square in the quilt above is signed "Mary Jones" and dated 1795. It is rare to find an 18th-century pieced quilt; rarer still is one that is also embroidered and dated.

Embroidery has always been linked with American quilts, although it has generally been used for embellishment rather than as the foundation of a design.

Antique quilts that feature embroidery as overall or repeat patterns are extremely rare. Not only were thread and floss for sewing and embroidery scarce in the days of the early colonies, but quilting and embroidery required leisure time that usually was not available. While either quilting or embroidery might be used for a bedcover, the two were seldom combined in one.

When embroidery was used to embellish 18th-century quilts, it was apt to reflect the influence of imported Indian textiles and often depicted the same motifs, such as flowering branches and the tree of life. *Broderie perse* quilts, for example, were usually appliquéd with motifs cut directly from printed Indian cottons. These appliqués—delicately rendered and shaded leaves, flowers, and birds—may have been thought of as a way to imitate embroidery (thus

Embroidered Quilts

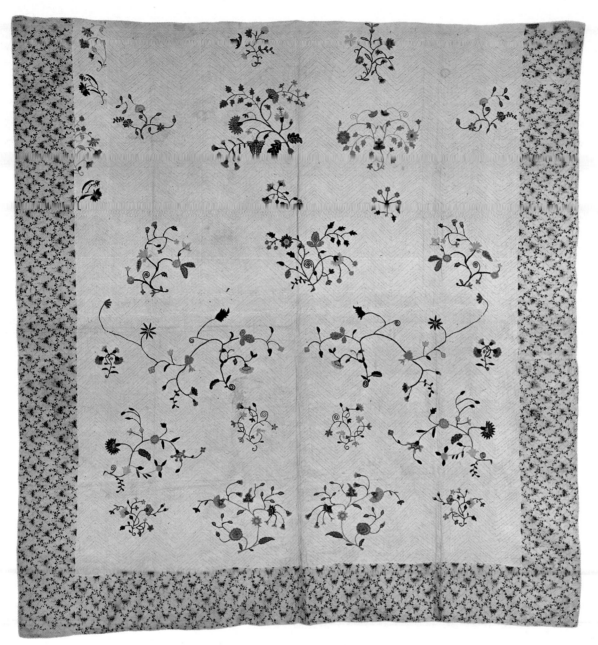

The tambourwork floral sprigs on the linen quilt at left resemble the flowering branches printed on 18th-century Indian textiles. Fine, handspun worsted yarn was used for the embroidery. The quilt is signed and dated "Mildred, Cos Cob, Rhy, 1753."

avoiding the actual labor). Still, some *broderie perse* quilts occasionally have embroidered stitches in addition to the appliqués.

The American fascination with Indian designs also prompted an interest in a type of oriental embroidery called tambourwork. This technique involves stretching fabric over a tambour (drum-shaped) frame and pulling embroidery thread up through the weave with a needle-thin hook. The thread is then looped into minute chain stitches that outline the designs; repeated rows of these stitches are also used to fill in and shade flowers and leaves. Like other types of embroidered quilts, those decorated with tambourwork are exceedingly rare, and are prized by collectors.

It was not until the Victorian era that embroidered quilts finally became common. From 1860 to 1900, decorative embroidery stitches were used extensively for borders and pictorial subjects on fancy silk quilts. This was the one period in American quilting when no quilt was complete without such an ornamental touch.

Unique Embroidered Quilts

The one-of-a-kind wool quilt above is called a Blackboard quilt because of its dark background and its colorful embroidered designs, which resemble chalk drawings.

The embroidery on some quilts stands out as unique American folk art. In the example above, called a Blackboard quilt, the bright cotton outline stitches on the black wool background resemble line drawings rather than traditional embroidery designs. Curiously, the design stitched to the left of center depicts a pieced-quilt pattern. The two women whose names appear with the date 1906 may have made the quilt together: no one knows why "Doll See Me" was stitched in one corner.

On the wool quilt at right, made between 1815 and 1830, the embroidered squares were stitched together like appliqué blocks. The whimsical flowers and vibrant colors give the quilt a lively, original look; the use of sashes around the blocks is unusual for wool quilts of that period.

The maker of the quilt
at left seems to have given
herself the challenge of
embroidering every kind of
flowerpot she could imagine.
Made between 1815 and
1830, the quilt combines
a turn-of-the-century
embroidery style with
a slightly later style
of sash.

Tied Quilts

Forming a scallop pattern, the colored knots used in tying the early-20th-century Afro-American quilt above provide a contrast for the vibrant piecing.

The term "quilt" includes several types of pieced bedcovers that are held together by means other than quilting. Tied quilts are one such type—their name refers to the technique of tying together the layers of fabric in a quilt with yarn or a thick strand of embroidery floss. Done at reasonably close intervals, tying is all that is required to keep the batting in place.

The technique is typically used in quilts that are meant to serve as everyday blankets and that must stand up to constant wear and washing. It is also favored by women who enjoy piecing quilt tops but do not have the time or inclination to spend hours on intricate quilting.

Tying has other practical purposes: quilts that are interlined with blankets or other thick padding, for instance, are usually too heavy to

be quilted. Similarly, certain pieced-quilt tops, such as the Log Cabin pattern and most varieties of crazy quilt, are too thick to be quilted in the traditional manner and are often tied instead.

Tying can also be decorative. A quilt that is pieced with fabrics in busy prints is often enhanced by tying: white or bright-colored yarns add contrasting pattern where fine quilting might not show at all. Some solid-color pieced-quilt patterns, such as Baby Blocks, also benefit from tying, since the knots become part of the overall design and add textural interest.

The bold, asymmetrical designs of Afro-American quilts, as in the examples shown here, are also often complemented with tying. In the quilt opposite, the knots are placed in scalloped rows to imitate a similar quilting pattern; above, they punctuate the geometric pieced design.

The quilter's careful use of tied knots enhances the graphic design of the Afro-American quilt above and contributes to the unique charm of the piece.

Victorian
Silk Quilts

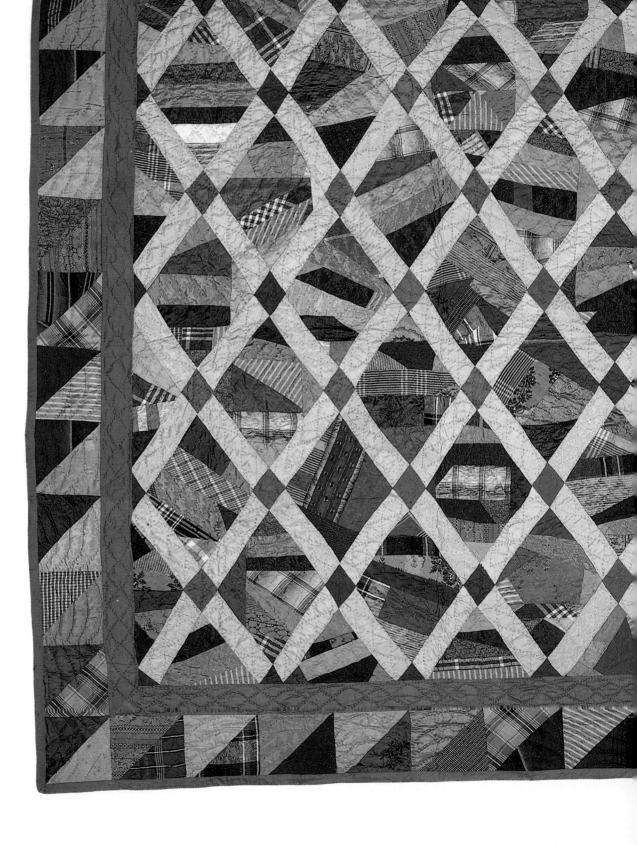

*Like more traditional quilts,
the silk quilt at right, made
in New York State about
1870, consists of blocks and
sashes. Pieced "crazy"
patches like those in the
interior blocks here would
become especially popular in
the decade to follow.*

American quilts frequently reflect the changes in women's fashions as well as the development of the nation's textile industry. During the Victorian era, for example, this country began producing nearly as much silk as it imported, and from the 1860s to 1900, quilts made from silk dress fabric were the rage.

Along with the new quilt fabric came new designs, which ensured that silk quilts would look nothing like their "old-fashioned" cotton cousins. Rather than simply replicating the clearly defined patterns that characterized many earlier quilts, Victorian quilters tended to combine colors and prints in ways that resembled stained-glass windows or kaleidoscope views. Patterns based on pieced strips, such as the herringbone, became extremely popular. Other designs relied on single repeating shapes, like diamonds or hexagons, for a striking effect.

Unless they had plain borders, colorful silk quilts were rarely used to display fancy quilting stitches, thus few silk quilts are actually quilted. More often they are tied, or stitched just enough to keep the layers of fabric in place.

Early Victorian silk quilts, like the 1858 Pennsylvania pieced example above, are usually far more subtle in color and design than quilts from later in that era.

A Crazy Phase

Stitched by Susan McCord in Indiana around 1880, the crazy quilt at left is made of wool scraps decorated with embroidery. Each of the "wheels" in this unique quilt is actually four pieced fans joined together.

Throughout the Victorian era, nearly every aspect of furnishing the home was influenced by a new awareness of foreign cultures. Decorative motifs that seemed exotic or slightly bizarre to 19th-century eyes were quickly incorporated into designs for wallpaper, fabrics, and even quilts.

Between 1875 and 1900, for example, crazy quilts—in which no two patches looked alike—coincided with the arrival of Japanese prints and screens in America. The asymmetrical designs and liberal use of ornamental gilt in these oriental artworks had a strong influence on crazy-quilt designs.

The aim of crazy quilts was to join unrelated shapes of fabric in as decorative a manner as possible: seams were finished with fancy stitches; beadwork and spangles were added for sparkle; patches were painted and embroidered.

Typically, crazy quilts were made by sewing the patches onto a large piece of cloth that was then backed with pretty fabric and given a decorative border. Whenever possible, silks and velvets were used, although the selection in rural areas was often limited to cotton and wool. Manufacturers capitalized on the fad by offering assortments of silk pieces and complete crazy-quilt kits, available by mail order.

Silk squares depicting popular figures were given away as tobacco premiums around 1900. Among the personalities in the crazy quilt opposite are George Washington and Buffalo Bill.

Embroidered Silk Quilts

Fancy embroidery stitches highlight the pieced fans in the quilt above, made around 1890. Using fans for quilt motifs reflected the Victorian fascination with Japanese culture.

Even after the craze for crazy quilts began to fade, around 1890, needleworkers continued to embellish the more restrained-patterned silk quilts that came into vogue, adding elaborate embroidery stitched in silk and metallic threads. Few women devised their own embroidery designs, however; most were traced or transferred from patterns in magazines. Kits containing embroidery floss and prestamped silks could also be purchased.

There were dozens of popular stitches: herringbone, feather, and buttonhole were among the most common for borders. Some of the more pictorial designs were executed as simple outlines, others were filled in with realistically stitched shadows, highlights, and details. Any type of flower or animal motif was popular; owls and other birds, spider webs, and pictures of children from Kate Greenaway's illustrated books were also favorites.

The simply outlined flowers that embellish the silk quilt above are typical of the embroidered motifs favored in the 1890s, when this New Hampshire quilt was made.

A
Pastel
Revival

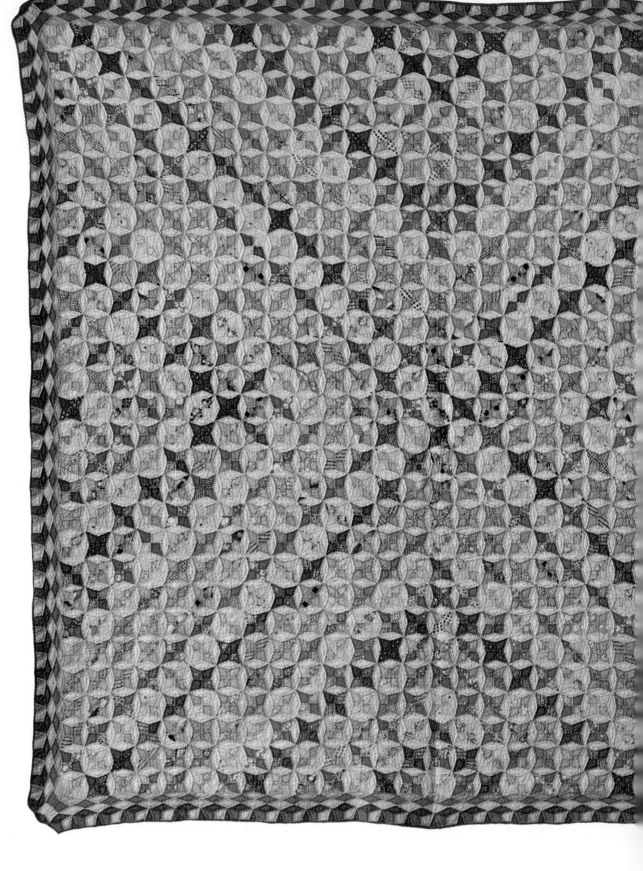

During the 1930s many
traditional quilt patterns,
such as the World Without
End pattern of the quilt at
right, were reinterpreted in
pastel colors; the pink,
mint green, yellow, and
lavender in this example
are typical.

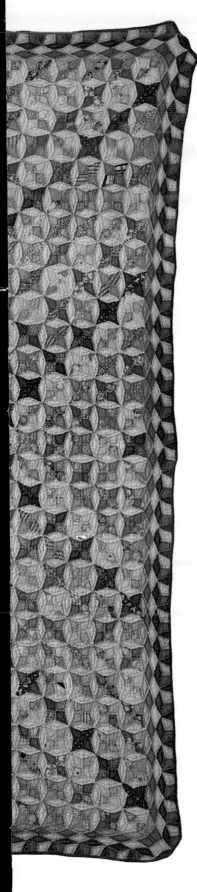

By 1900 most American women were purchasing their bedcovers, and quilts fell out of fashion. With the onset of the Depression in the late 1920s, however, economic concerns brought on a revival of quiltmaking.

The distinctive quilts of that period can be recognized by their pastel colors—the antithesis of the dark shades favored in the Victorian era and an antidote to hard times. Although many traditional patterns were revived in the 1930s, new ones were devised as well, and "novelty" patterns that made innovative use of fabric scraps also became popular.

Depression-era quilts were copied from patterns printed in newspapers and magazines, and some were made from kits that came with pre-stamped fabric ready to be cut and sewn. Among the most beautiful quilts of the period were those made with floral appliqués and finished with elaborate quilting. The patterns included pansies, irises, and morning glories—flowers that never appeared on 19th-century quilts.

The floral appliqué quilts of the 1920s and 1930s, such as the Morning Glory example above, often had beautifully quilted white backgrounds. Many women gave their completed appliqués to professionals who did the actual quilting, charging by the yard of thread used.

Maverick
Quilts

Eagle quilts, such as the example above, were popular during the late 19th century, but this is the only one known to have been made in black.

Although the work of every quilter is personalized by individual choices of fabrics and stitches, the patterns and color schemes quilters select are often standard. Occasionally, however, "maverick" quilts are found that offer surprising new twists on traditional themes. Today we can only guess whether the needleworkers who created such quilts set out to make one-of-a-kind statements or were simply being playful.

Quilts with appliquéd eagles became particularly popular after the 1876 Centennial in Philadelphia, when the design above was made available as a kit. The highly unusual color

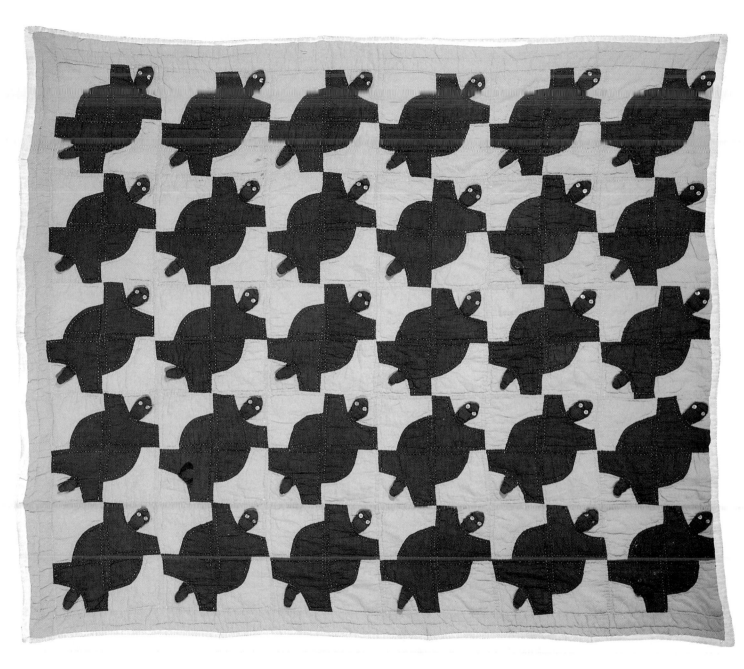

scheme and center medallion in this quilt, however, mark it as a personal adaptation. Because Amish and Mennonite quilters were the only people who used large areas of black fabric in their quilts at that time, it is believed that a member of one of these religious sects borrowed the pattern from an "English" neighbor and adapted it to reflect her own color preferences.

The maker of the red silk and white cotton pieced quilt above rearranged the basic pieces that make up the traditional Drunkard's Path pattern, and came up with Turtles instead. The stuffed heads and tails and the button eyes were added separately, probably to delight a child.

Made in the South in the late 19th or early 20th century, the Turtles quilt above is a unique design adapted from a traditional pieced pattern.

New
Directions

The quilter's choice of
pattern, fabric, and details
gives the quilt at right a far
more personal design than is
found in most quilts. The
well-defined buildings may
even be copies of those in an
actual community.

Some makers of maverick quilts may start with an idea inspired by a traditional pattern, but by the time they finish they will have created an original design.

The basic Schoolhouse pattern used for the quilt above has been popular since the 1870s. Believed to have originated in New Jersey, it is one of the few pictorial designs that is customarily pieced rather than appliquéd.

In typical variations on the Schoolhouse pattern, quilters often incorporate churches or cottages in repeating blocks. For the maverick quilt at left, however—made in Massachusetts in the late 19th century—the quilter included the basic schoolhouse only once in her design and used no repeating blocks. Although pieced in a similar way to the Schoolhouse pattern, each of the blocks in this quilt has been individualized and may even record the actual houses and barns in the quiltmaker's community.

Designed during the 1870s, the Schoolhouse quilt above combines a nostalgic theme with bright, clean design. One of the best-loved quilt designs, this pattern has many variations.

Cultural Expressions

history, politics, religion, friendship, and stories in quilts

Throughout much of American history, quilts have answered many needs beyond those of warmth and comfort. A reflection of a woman's skill with a needle, a quilt could also be a testament to her social conscience, religious beliefs, and cultural background.

During the 19th century, an age when the average woman's life centered on domestic affairs and idleness was considered the "devil's playground," quilting provided a welcome outlet for individual expression. Although a woman could not vote, she could still cast a symbolic ballot for a favored candidate with a political quilt. In addition, quilts were used to raise funds, to champion civic causes, and to voice protests against war and slavery. As "paintings" in fabrics, they recorded local scenes and told stories. And adorned with familiar images and the names of loved ones, they helped commemorate important occasions or express esteem and affection. Such quilts are cherished not only for their fine craftsmanship, but also for the strong sentiments they convey.

Shown in a detail, a quilt commemorates the 1933 Chicago Century of Progress Exhibition.

Album
Quilts

Several of the blocks in the circa 1850 album quilt at right are thought to be made by Mary Evans, an accomplished Baltimore needle-worker and professional quilter. The art of the album quilt reached its height during the pre-Civil War era in Baltimore, then an affluent city where many women had ready access to the best domestic and imported fabrics.

During the mid-1800s, there was a vogue for a type of block quilt known as an album quilt in which each block featured an individual "textile picture." Typically, the image was a floral wreath or bouquet, basket, fruit, lovebirds, or a picture that would have sentimental meaning for the owner. The blocks—usually appliquéd, but sometimes pieced—might all be made by the same person, or individual blocks might be stitched, and perhaps signed, by many different needleworkers.

Album quilts were almost always designed as gifts, perhaps to commemorate a birth or wedding, or to express esteem for a community figure, such as an admired clergyman or teacher. When made for a special person or occasion, album quilts were also called friendship or presentation quilts.

Among the most highly regarded album quilts are those that were designed between 1846 and 1852 by two well-known Baltimore needlewomen, Mary Evans and Achsah Goodwin Wilkins. Extremely sophisticated, "Baltimore quilts" exhibit exceptional workmanship and often feature multilayered appliqué for realistic shading and texture.

Album quilts, like the small one above made around 1862 for a child, were often designed to mark children's births and birthdays.

Signature
Quilts

S ignature—or autograph—quilts are distinguished by the collections of names that were stamped, stenciled, inked, or stitched onto the quilt tops. Many, signed by family members or friends, served as keepsakes and reminders of loved ones. During the 1800s, such friendship quilts were often carried westward by women settling far from home on the frontier.

Other signature quilts were designed specifically to raise funds for such causes as war relief and missionary efforts or to promote social reform. Typically, community members would pay a small sum—from five cents to five dollars—to have their names included on a quilt, which was then sold at a church or community function.

Made in the Chimney Sweep pattern, the friendship quilt above features names worked in embroidery thread. On the 1070 fund-raising quilt at right, the nearly one thousand signatures were added in indelible ink, first available in the 1830s.

CONTINUING A TRADITION

As more has become known about the powerful means of self-expression that 19th-century needleworkers found in their quilts, contemporary needleworkers have been newly inspired to continue the tradition. Today, as in the past, quilts are being made to demonstrate patriotic sentiments, interest in current events, or perhaps esteem for a school, church, community, or an individual.

The quilt at top right, for example, celebrates both the centennial and bicentennial of America. The center block was created by a quiltmaker caught up in the patriotism of 1876. For some reason, the quilt remained unfinished until it was taken up again two generations later by the quilter's great-nephew. Using the original fabric pieces, which had been saved, he added the border in time for the nation's 200th birthday.

The quilt at bottom right was made by parents and teachers for a fund-raising auction at a school in New York City. Each block depicts a school-related activity, such as reading or soccer practice, or a local scene. The ornate border re-creates the New York skyline, including

Quilts can express their "meaning" symbolically or literally. The patriotic quilt at top uses a variety of stylized red, white, and blue star and flag motifs to pay tribute to America. The fund-raiser quilt at bottom is a pictorial record of scenes and activities that had special meaning for a New York City school.

such landmarks as the Brooklyn Bridge and the Statue of Liberty.

The quilt at top left was inspired by 19th-century signature quilts, which were often designed to raise money: people would pay to have their names stitched or inked onto the quilt top. In an effort to help the Flushing, Michigan, historical society transform an old train depot into a museum, the maker of this quilt suggested that space for signatures on the "bricks" and "spokes" of the border be sold to members of the community. The center panels of the quilt depict city landmarks, including the first school and church, and of course, the train station.

The idea for the quilt at bottom left was derived from the "freedom quilt," a type of album quilt that was traditionally given in the late 18th and early 19th centuries to a young man when he turned twenty-one. The quilt collector who commissioned this one for her son worked with a professional quiltmaker to design the different blocks. The appliquéd pictures record the young man's hobbies, the schools he attended, and even some of his favorite television shows.

The quilt at top was made for a Michigan town's sesquicentennial celebration. Funds were raised for the local historical society by selling signature space on the border "bricks" for $3, and on the wheel "spokes" for $15. The album quilt at bottom was made as a 21st birthday gift for a young man.

57

Patriotic Quilts

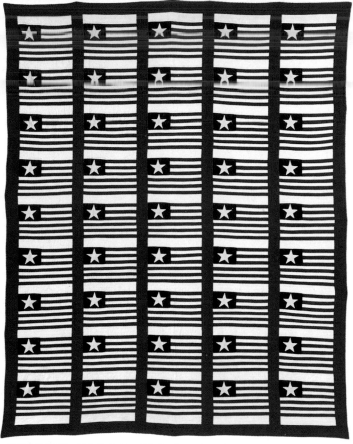

American quilts with patriotic themes are as old as the nation itself; the first examples date back to the era of the Revolution. Over time, such events as a war, a state's admission to the Union, or a presidential inauguration have all provided inspiration for quiltmakers. By making quilts in patterns with names like President's Wreath and White House Steps, Kansas Beauty and California Poppy, women expressed their loyalty to country and state.

Naturally, many patriotic quilts from all periods are decorated with the stars and stripes and in the red, white, and blue color scheme of the American flag. Even more popular than the flag motif are patterns based on the star alone, which had myriad variations.

Patriotic patterns also feature such images as eagles, shields, and the Statue of Liberty, as well as passages from hymns and patriotic songs. Commemorative handkerchiefs printed with presidential portraits, famous battle scenes, maps, and familiar historic buildings were also frequently sewn into quilts.

Strips of solid-color and polka-dot fabrics make up the stylized stars in the circa 1930 quilt above left. Flags, like those on the quilt above right, were particularly popular for quilts during wartime.

The quilt opposite was exhibited at the Centennial Exposition in Philadelphia. It features two flags: one has 13 stars for the original colonies, the other has 38 for the states in the Union in 1876.

O ver the years, political quilts have been made not only to champion controversial causes, like woman suffrage and emancipation, but also to express support of candidates and parties. Such quilts might also relate an opinion about an event of national significance or a new government program.

The quilt above, for example, made near the end of World War II, is a tribute to the men who lost their lives at Pearl Harbor. Depicted in the Vs for victory—also spelled out in Morse code— are Allied leaders Roosevelt, Churchill, and Stalin, as well as MacArthur; the American eagle, the British bulldog, and the Russian bear are shredding enemy flags. Flags of some of the Allied nations—including Britain, Russia, Australia, and China—adorn the border.

The quilt at right endorses the Townsend Plan, a 1930s proposal to pay every citizen over age sixty $200 per month—a generous sum in an era when the average monthly income per capita was around $40.

Sewn by a Welsh immigrant in 1945, the quilt above was made to keep the memory of Pearl Harbor alive. The pansies symbolize remembrance.

Political Quilts

The South Dakota merchants and employees who "signed" the quilt at left in the 1930s used the signature quilt as a kind of fabric petition to support the Townsend Old Age Plan. The quilt is stitched with such provocative slogans as "A nation is known by its treatment of youth and of its aged."

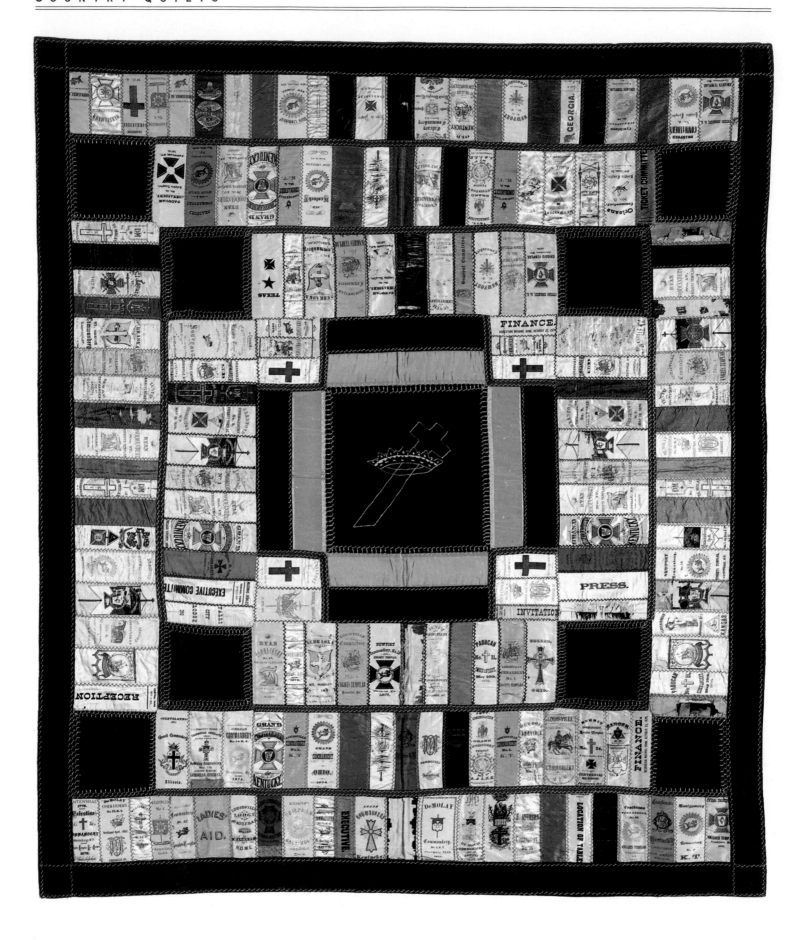

Ribbon Quilts

The circa 1890 quilt at left was made from ribbons saved from political campaigns waged earlier in the century. Such quilts were sometimes made as records of campaigns in which the quiltmakers had been involved.

Popular in the late 1800s, ribbon quilts were an offshoot of the fad for crazy quilts. Victorian quilters often augmented their supplies of silk and velvet scraps with printed ribbons, including souvenirs, prize ribbons from country fairs, or premiums offered in cigar and cigarette packets. The quilt opposite comprises ribbons collected from Masonic meetings and conventions, and may have been a tribute to someone's involvement in the order. In the quilt above, the central panel features political campaign ribbons from the mid-1800s.

Made around 1890, the Masonic ribbon quilt opposite features the same type of fancy embroidery as the crazy quilts of the period. The cross-and-crown motif is a symbol used by the order.

THE QUILTING BEE

J ust as a quilt joined pieces of fabric, a quilting bee brought women together. Popular mainly from the mid-1700s through the 1930s—although the tradition is still carried on today—bees were so named for the industriousness of the participants. Ostensibly held to stitch together the layers of a quilt, bees in fact offered much more: they provided a break from the monotony of farm work and the isolation of rural life, and they gave women a chance to help themselves while helping others as well.

Since the lives of women revolved around work, and idle socializing was frowned upon, bees allowed needleworkers to enjoy one another's company and still have something constructive to show for their time. A woman eagerly awaited an invitation to a quilting bee: it was a sign of her acceptance in a group and an acknowledgment of her skills.

The woman hosting a bee scrubbed her house, made sure her own quilts were displayed, and prepared plenty of food. The quilt tops were set up on frames and women sat close together on all sides. Fingers flew as tongues wagged: news and gossip were passed along, recipes exchanged, and the trials of children and marriage discussed. No wonder suffragist Susan B. Anthony delivered her first equal rights speech at a quilting bee, where women had always been able to voice their views without censure.

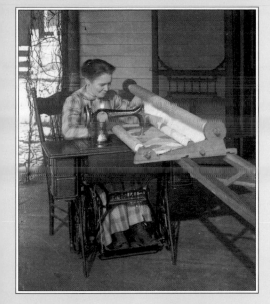

Bees drew women of all backgrounds and ages; the shared experience turned strangers into friends and bridged social and generational gaps. Here young girls learned what would be expected of them in womanhood, and smaller children got a taste of "work" as they stood by to thread needles.

Sometimes bees were held for special reasons: perhaps to announce an engagement and prepare a future bride's traditional thirteen quilts for her dowry, or to make a friendship quilt for a neighbor who was moving. Often a bee would be followed by a "frolic" to celebrate a job well done.

It is not surprising that quilting bees are still held today. Contemporary quiltmakers find these gatherings just as congenial for finishing a quilt—whether the piece be for personal use, for a gift, or for a political or social cause—as did the generations of women before them.

Top, left to right: a Connecticut girl learns piecework at the turn of the century; women at a bee in Oregon, c. 1905; quilting with a treadle-powered machine, c. 1914; New England children working quilt blocks in the late 1800s. **Bottom, left to right:** a New England quilting bee; quilting in the 20th century; Louisiana Cajun women finishing a central medallion quilt, c. 1930; a Pennsylvania nonagenarian quilting for her church; an 1849 "social" bee.

Pictorial Quilts

A s late as the Victorian era, women's opportunities for imaginative self-expression outside the home were still quite limited. Even in quilting, most women were bound by tradition. Although an individual might make a hundred quilts in her lifetime, her works generally tended to repeat the same standard piecing and appliqué patterns.

An exception, however, was the pictorial quilt, a kind of "painting" in fabric that told a story or depicted a scene from literature, the Bible, or the life of the quiltmaker. Most pictorial quilts were made in the late 1800s, when quilts began to become more of an accessory than a necessity. These remarkable textiles reflected an innovative, self-confident leap beyond the norm and were considered masterpieces of needlework: not every quiltmaker could conceive entire scenes in fabric, let alone execute them skillfully.

The quilt at right, made in 1872 by an Ohio woman as a gift to her granddaughter, is a faithful yet witty record of life in the needleworker's rural township. The quilt is all the more charming for its lack of pretense: the maker captured "real" people—not heroic or religious figures—engaged in such everyday activities as churning butter, driving a buggy, taking a walk, plowing a field, and milking a cow.

This elaborate pictorial quilt was made in 1872 by Phoebe Cook of Edison Township in Morrow County, Ohio. Using fabric like paint, the quiltmaker produced a remarkable work of art, distinguished for its realistic—and animated— interpretation of the human form.

Crazy Pictures

Made primarily of wool, the 1898 pictorial crazy quilt above features an assortment of small-town characters, including children, haughty matrons, and dapper businessmen.

These two 19th-century quilts combine pictorial content with the crazy-quilt form. In the example above, the maker used randomly pieced blocks to form a background for a group of individualized portraits depicting some of the residents in her Delaware County, New York, township. The costumes on the figures are skillfully rendered in three dimensions: jackets overlay shirts and trousers, skirts are gracefully draped, and bustles and leg-of-mutton sleeves puff out appropriately.

The quilt opposite captures twelve scenes from the maker's coastal Massachusetts hometown. The intricately embroidered scenes demonstrate fine needlework, despite the charmingly distorted perspective.

The mid-1800s quilt opposite was started by Celestine Bacheller when she was sixteen. The daughter of a silk dyer, she seems to have taken full advantage of her access to fine fabrics.

Bible Quilts

With religion a powerful influence in 19th-century life, women naturally turned to the Bible for inspiration for their quilt designs. Quiltmakers often incorporated scriptural stories and quotations into their creations, and patterns with such names as Jacob's Ladder, Job's Tears, and Crown of Thorns abounded.

The pictorial Bible quilts shown here were both made in the 1890s. The primitive quilt op-posite celebrates a number of sacred events, including Jesus and John the Baptist meeting at the River Jordan and Christ praying in the garden.

The quilt above, made by a former slave named Harriet Powers, illustrates such events as the temptation of Adam and Eve, Jonah being swallowed by the whale, and the Crucifixion. It also recounts local occurrences that the maker felt showed God's hand at work, among them an 1833 meteor shower.

Harriet Powers, an ex-slave, made the Bible quilt above around 1895, but was later forced by hard times to sell it. She occasionally called on the buyer "to visit the darling offspring of her brain."

The Pennsylvania maker of the circa 1895 "Sacret Bibel" quilt, opposite, penciled messages onto cotton labels and sewed them to the quilt to explain the joyous scenes she had stitched.

The pattern of the quilt above, from the Arthur, Illinois, Amish community, is based on the diamond, a standard motif that has religious meaning for the sect.

Amish Quilts

Amish quilts are a reflection of the tenets of this fundamentalist Germanic sect, whose members settled in Pennsylvania in the 1720s and had spread through the Midwest by the early 1900s. The so-called Plain People, who still live in the same regions today, base their culture on piety, self-sufficiency, and separation from "the world," rejecting the modern, the superfluous, and the frivolous.

The strict order that applies to all aspects of Amish life is clearly evident in Amish quiltmaking, which had its heyday from around 1870 to 1935. Always pieced, these early quilts generally consist of three simple, geometric shapes and are made of wool or cotton. Originally, the shapes had a symbolic meaning—the diamond, for example, has a religious significance for the Amish—but the quilts themselves were never

Continued

The circa 1910 quilt above is worked in Diamond in the Square, one of the most common patterns used for quilts by the Amish of Lancaster County, Pennsylvania.

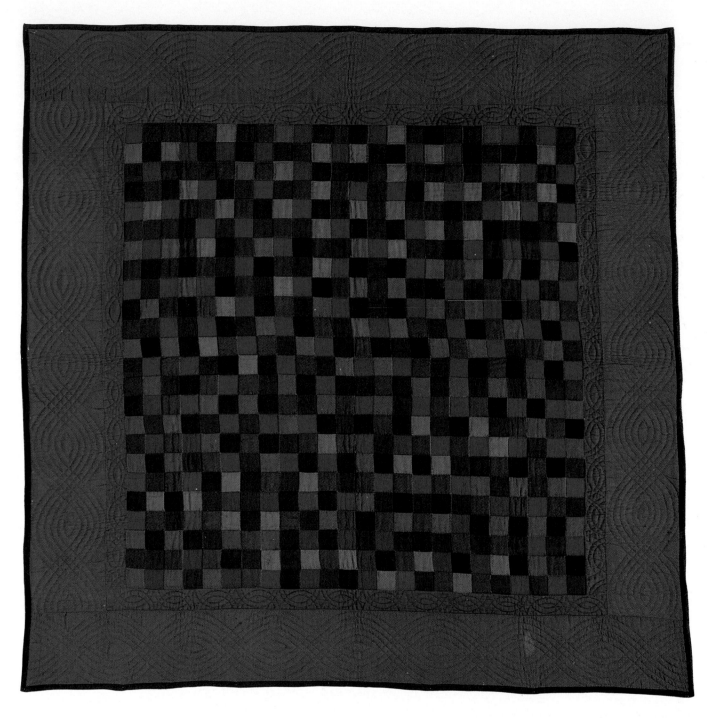

Amish quilts that juxtapose light and dark squares, as in the 1930s example above, are said to reflect the dichotomy existing between the Amish and the outside world.

made as anything other than practical furnishings. Amish quilting patterns show greater variation than the piecing patterns, often including a variety of Christian symbols, such as the rose and a popularized form of the lily, the tulip.

Although the sect does not permit using figured, checked, or even dotted fabrics for either clothing or quilt tops, a relatively wide choice of colors is used. Much in the same way that the Amish pair somber-colored outer garments with dresses, aprons, and shirts in vibrant shades of purple, green, and turquoise, Amish women often combine bright and dark colors in their quilts. The surprising, sometimes shocking,

juxtaposition of colors, which often appear to glow, reveals an energy that seems to belie the subdued lifestyle associated with the sect.

Amish quilts tend to vary in both design and color from region to region. Those from Lancaster County, Pennsylvania—the location of the first and most conservative Amish commu-

nity—generally exhibit traditional patterns and quiet colors. Quilts made later, in the midwestern settlements, are freer in design and color, and often incorporate yellow and black into the designs. Many of today's Amish quilts are sewn with synthetic fabric, but they are still characterized by traditional designs.

The maker of the circa 1920 Ohio quilt above devised an unusual pattern in which 288 small square blocks make up 72 circles—a difficult quilt to piece.

H awaiian quilts, clearly unnecessary for warmth in the tropical climate of the islands, are something of a curiosity. Sewing itself was little known in Hawaii before the 19th century; the Hawaiians used paper-like "fabrics" made from pounded bark. It was not until the first American missionary ship landed in 1820 that native women, eager to emulate Western customs, took up needlework. They soon began copying American techniques, using them to interpret in fabric the same patterns that distinguished the pounded bark.

The unique figural quilt above is a striking example of the blend of native myth and the religion taught by the Christian missionaries. Here, two characters from a romantic Hawaiian legend—the supernatural hero Eleanale and the earthly princess Leinaala—are juxtaposed with those of Adam and Eve in Eden.

The quilt at right displays a typical Hawaiian quiltmaking technique: a single piece of cloth is folded and cut freehand to create a symmetrical design evocative of the native flora. The cutout is then appliquéd onto a contrasting ground.

Based on the myth of Eleanale and Leinaala, the subject of the first native-language literary work to be published in the Hawaiian Islands, the early-1900s quilt above also includes Adam and Eve.

Hawaiian Quilts

The design of the 1940 floral
quilt at left includes a
needlework technique that is
unique to Hawaii—outlining
the appliqué pattern with
repeated rows of fine stitches.
Appropriately called "echo
quilting," such stitching is
said to recall the waves
of the ocean.

THREE

Pattern and Design

reflecting infinite variations
in fabric, color, and scale

No two quilts are ever exactly alike. The individual character of each is affected not only by the quality of the needlework, but by the quiltmaker's choice of construction technique, fabric, color, pattern, quilting design, backing, and finishing details.

Passed down through generations, many of the same pattern motifs—the star, the basket, the wedding ring, for instance—have been used over and over, but even these favorites can look entirely different when worked by different hands. In some patterns, such as those based on the star, the motif itself often varies in design. In others, such as the Log Cabin or Grandmother's Flower Garden pattern, a particular fabric type or combination of colors can create unusual effects even though the pattern itself never changes. Pattern names—inspired by nature, household objects, wallpaper prints—vary as much as the designs. What is known as the Star of Bethlehem in one part of the country, for example, might be called Star of the East or Lone Star in another. As shown in the following pages, it is this diversity that provides much of the pleasure in quiltmaking and quilt collecting.

A detail of an Amish Double Patch quilt displays deft handling of color.

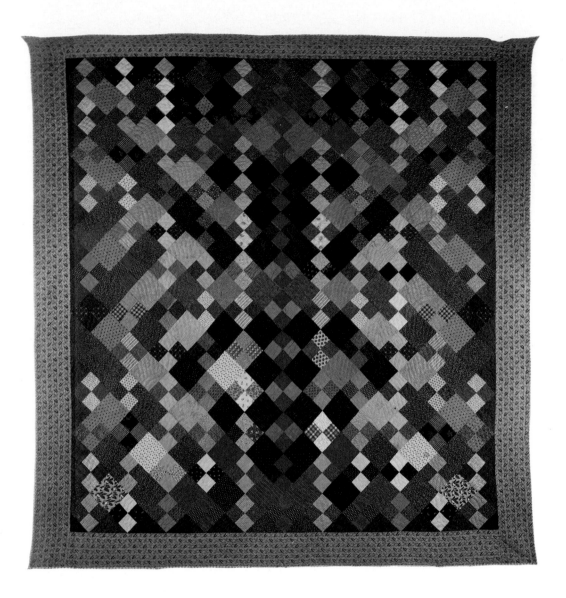

The fabric square, or patch, is an elementary design unit in quiltmaking. Two fundamental types of patch constructions are the four patch, in which a quilt square is composed of four smaller, same-size squares, and the nine patch, in which a quilt square is composed of nine smaller, same-size squares. To make the smaller patches, squares of different fabrics are carefully cut and then reassembled so that the colors and prints are mixed in a new square. The placement of the patches and the varied fabric patterns determine the overall design.

Patch patterns are favored by beginning quiltmakers because the straight seams are easy to stitch. Yet, when arranged with skill and combined with other quilt patterns, patches can be worked into sophisticated designs. The makers of the Four Patch quilt above and the Nine Patch quilt at right were meticulous about choosing specific fabrics and then placing them carefully to evoke a sense of energy and depth in these bedcovers.

The Four Patch quilt above, made around 1895, is simple in design, yet the mix of printed and solid

fabrics in dark and light shades creates a dramatic effect.

Patch
Patterns

In the New York quilt at left, 25 nine-patch squares are included in a pattern known as Chimneys and Cornerstones: the nine-patch squares represent the chimneys.

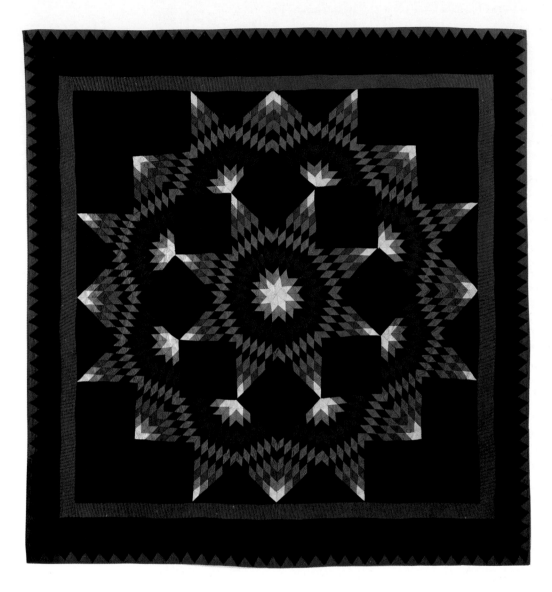

Probably no patterns are more popular for quilts than those based on the star, a motif that appears in both pieced and appliquéd works. The star is appealing in part because it is such a familiar symbol—of patriotism, hope, even romance. The simple, geometric shapes in star patterns can also make the designs surprisingly easy to draft and put together if the proper piecing system is used.

More than a hundred star designs are known.

The simplest star form is the Variable Star, which consists of a single square with eight triangular points. Other traditional stars generally have five and six points. In some patterns, the stars are used as multiples; in others, they are worked as a single, central star that radiates across the quilt top. Composed of thousands of small diamonds, both of the central-star patterns shown here are variations on the simple LeMoyne Star, an early quilt motif made of eight diamonds.

The Broken Star quilt pattern, above, is composed of a star within a star, creating the impression of a

star exploding. This Amish example, made from cotton sateen, was sewn around 1920.

Star Patterns

*The Star of Bethlehem, also
called the Blazing Star or
Lone Star, is among the most
intricate of star patterns.
The 1849 example at left is
made of more than forty-two
hundred pieces. In such
patterns, which are based on
a geometric progression, the
slightest error in cutting or
sewing one of the diamond
shapes will distort the
entire design.*

One of the most basic star patterns, the Variable Star or Simple Star, was often made with a combination of scraps and store-bought fabrics. The maker of this mid-19th-century example truly "varied" her stars by using a mixture of colorful cottons.

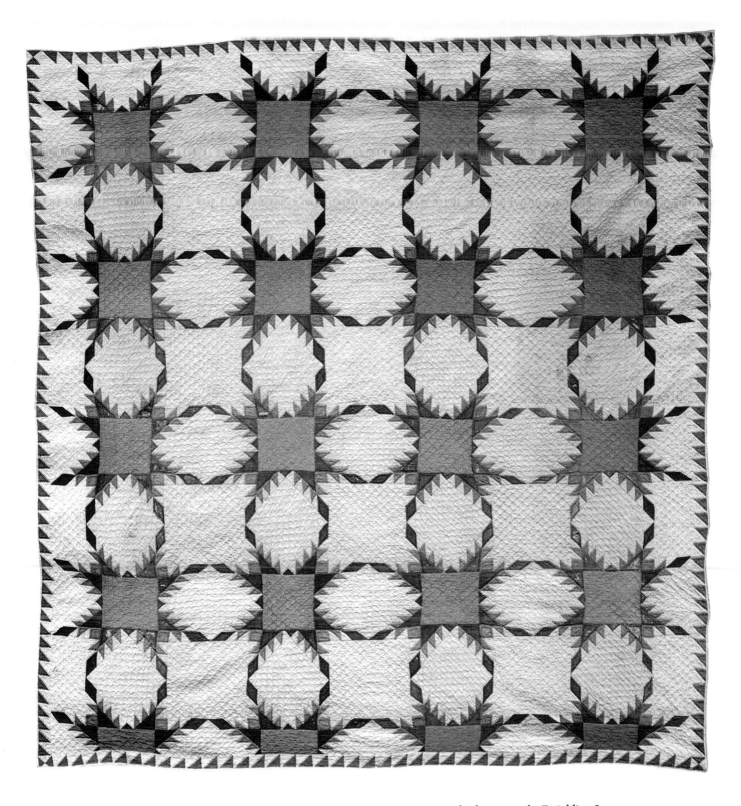

This late-19th-century quilt features the Feathered Star pattern—also known as the Twinkling Star
or the Sawtooth Star. In this pattern, small triangles and diamonds are added to the star points, creating
a delicate, seemingly "feathery" effect.

Basket Patterns

Striking variations on the basic basket motif include, clockwise from top left: the abstract Basket of Chips pattern; two different Cactus Baskets—so named for the spiked sawtooth handles; and a simple round-handled design.

Widely used since the mid-1800s, another quilt pattern motif is the basket. While the arrangement of baskets on a quilt top can vary considerably, the motif itself—which usually combines piecing and appliqué—is generally composed of triangles, or triangles and squares, sewn into an anvil-like shape. Often, a rounded or sawtooth handle is added; baskets without handles are unusual. Some baskets are empty; others hold flower and fruit appliqués, or are filled with abstract fabric shapes. Quilting stitches in floral or foliate patterns might also be used to suggest the contents of a basket.

With its simple, graphic appearance, the basket motif lends itself to original and effective designs. The baskets are often positioned opposite one another in symmetrical rows with the handles facing. In this way, there is no "wrong" direction to the overall pattern, and when such a quilt is placed on a bed, the baskets hanging over the sides appear to be right side up.

The maker of the 1860s cotton Basket quilt opposite arranged the baskets in a concentric pattern so that some of them would always appear upright. The baskets are pieced and the handles appliquéd.

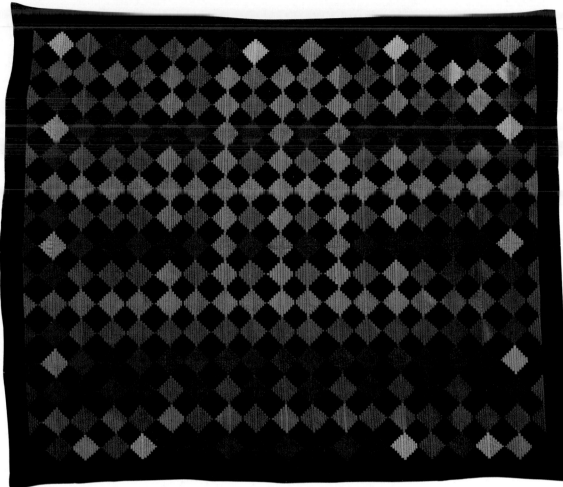

The Log Cabin was a popular pattern from the mid-1800s onward. In the Log Cabin—unlike in the Star and Basket patterns—the basic block form never changes; yet by using different colors and fabrics, the quiltmaker can achieve startling variations.

The quilt blocks in the Log Cabin pattern suggest the structure of the building for which it was named. Narrow fabric strips, or "logs," are laid in an interlocking pattern around a center square that represents the chimney or hearth: the square is almost always the same color (usually red, to symbolize warmth) throughout the quilt. Each block is constructed by first seaming strips to the sides of the center square, and then adding increasingly larger strips to each side until a block of the desired size is achieved. Each block must be carefully measured so that the edges of adjoining blocks match. Because of the large number of seams, Log Cabin quilts are seldom quilted; most are tacked or tied instead.

Early Log Cabin quilts were first made in wool and cotton, and later in the silks, satins, and velvets favored in the Victorian era. Regardless of the fabric used, the squares are always divided equally into two or four light and dark triangles. It is by varying the placement of these light and dark sections that needleworkers are able to create the striking optical illusions that distinguish many Log Cabin quilts.

While the structure of the Log Cabin block stayed the same, fabrics and colors might change according to fashion. The Light and Dark design in silk, above, was made during the Victorian era.

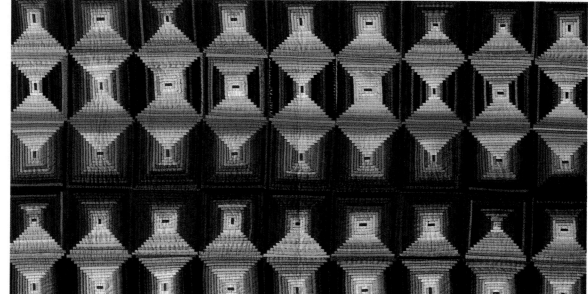

The distinctive looks of Log Cabin quilts depend on the particular arrangement of the light and dark triangles that make up the blocks. At right, the Barn Raising variation (top) creates the illusion of squares within squares. The Light and Dark design (middle) is distinguished by the unusual horizontal stripes that shoot across the quilt. In the Zigzag or Streak of Lightning design (bottom), dark zigzags frame colorful diamonds.

The primarily blue-and-white color scheme of the 1860s Log Cabin quilt above is unusual for the period.

This Barn Raising variation, with a Light and Dark border, is pieced from wool challis.

Log Cabin Variations

The striking colors and patterns displayed by the circa 1870 Windmill Blades quilt at right are enhanced by an equally dramatic sawtooth border.

Windmill Blades, also known as Pineapple, is a complicated variation of the Log Cabin pattern. Like other Log Cabin designs, this one took its names from familiar images: the water-pumping windmills that dotted the prairie during pioneer days, and the pineapple, which has been a symbol of hospitality since at least the 1700s.

In this design, the Log Cabin block consists of eight primary sections—four light and four dark —that alternate to give the illusion of spinning. The viewer's eye is constantly drawn from these moving "blades," to the contrasting background, to the circular and star shapes created by the overall pattern of light and dark. Because this design requires piecing that is far more precise than that needed for simpler Log Cabin patterns, Windmill Blades quilts are less commonly made.

By using a limited number of colors, the maker of the 1880s quilt above, which is thought to be

a Mennonite work, emphasized the graphic nature of the Windmill pattern. The ruffled border

is a typical Victorian touch.

Scale in Design

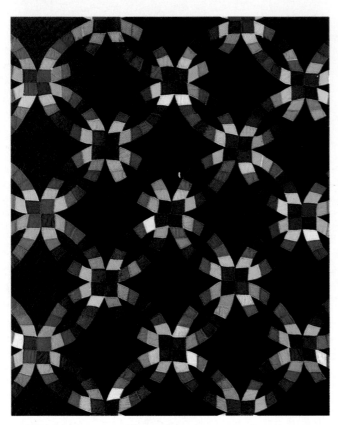

Variations in color scheme and scale create different effects in the two Double Wedding Ring designs above. Pieced with a dark cotton background, the smaller multicolored rings of the circa 1950 Ohio Amish example, left, seem to shimmer. Red and white patches accent the graphic look of the larger rings in the design at right.

The way a quilt looks is affected just as much by the scale of the design as by the choice of color and fabric. One pattern that changes dramatically when the scale is altered is the Double Wedding Ring, consisting of intersecting circles. The three Double Wedding Ring quilts shown here all measure roughly the same size and feature rows of between three and seven rings. The larger the rings, the more static the pattern appears; the smaller the rings, the more they seem to revolve.

It is unclear when the Double Wedding Ring pattern originated, but it became very popular in the 1920s with the advent of mail-order quilting kits, which included paper patterns and precut fabric swatches. A quilt made in the Double Wedding Ring pattern—the ring symbolized a never-ending bond—was not only a favorite gift for a bride but was also a valued addition to a young woman's hope chest.

Because curves are difficult to sew, many circular patterns, like the Double Wedding Ring, are pieced from wedge-shaped fabric patches to create the curves. The quiltmaker uses a template to cut the wedges, which are sewn together and then joined to large solid-color pieces— usually white—that are then embellished with fancy quilting designs.

Rectilinear borders are favored for Double Wedding Ring quilts because they make an effective frame for the circular patterns. Some Wedding Ring quilts, however, are finished along the curved pattern edges instead, creating a distinctive silhouette of scallops and points.

Even though she used scraps, the maker of the 1930s Double Wedding Ring quilt above demonstrated a fine sense of design by carefully choosing the colors. The "moving" rings are contained within a triple border that has Nine Patch squares at the corners.

Using cotton, the maker of the 1920s Grandmother's Flower Garden quilt above matched her fabrics
to define circular "flower beds" separated by white "paths."

Effects with Fabric

The same quilt pattern can look dramatically different when different types of fabric are used. The two quilts shown here were made in the Grandmother's Flower Garden pattern, also called Honeycomb or Mosaic. The pattern comprises hundreds of small hexagons that are first basted onto stiff paper templates and then whip-stitched together.

The Depression-era quilt opposite was made with simple pastel cottons that give the pattern a cheerful, casual feeling. The more formal Victorian quilt above, believed to have been started by a young boy during the Civil War, was pieced in dark silks favored for quiltmaking at the time.

According to family legend, the elegant quilt above was started by a Kentucky boy during the Civil War. It was not completed until 1907, as the corner date suggests.

Choosing Quilt Fabrics

Choosing fabrics is one of the greatest pleasures in quiltmaking. Some needleworkers prefer to use vintage remnants; others turn to their own workbaskets for scraps. But it is also possible to purchase new fabrics, like those shown at right, and still achieve a traditional look for a quilt.

Select colors and prints you like, but do so with care. Tightly woven fabrics are best: quilts made from fabrics that stretch or ravel easily will lose their shape. To test for tightness of weave, pull the fabric on the bias. If it doesn't return to shape quickly, be wary of using it.

It is also important to test each fabric for colorfastness. Do this by pre-washing a piece of the yardage in hot water and detergent; if the dye bleeds or streaks, don't use the fabric. Pre-washing also ensures that any shrinkage will occur *before* the quilt is made.

If you are using different materials in a quilt, choose those that are compatible. Don't combine silks, velvets, and other nonwashable fabrics with cottons and linens, which do not dry-clean well; and avoid mixing heavy and light fabrics such as denim and calico.

Clockwise from top left are new fabrics for five traditional quilt looks: pastels, popular in 1920s quilts; vivid Amish-style solids; homespuns; calicoes; and a variety of choices for crazy quilts.

Quilt Borders

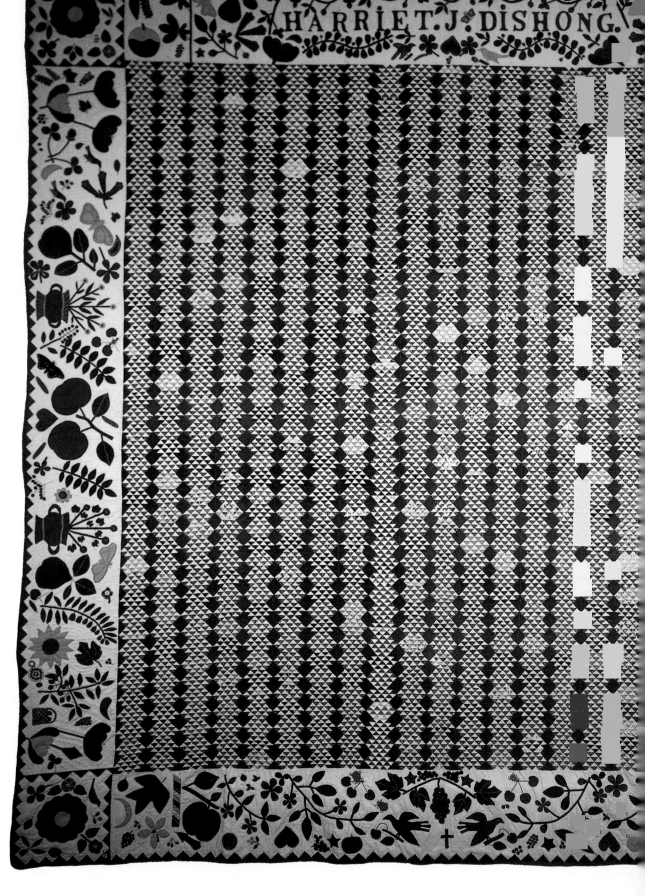

Made by Harriet J. Dishong with the help of her sister Mary, the quilt at right features an appliqué border that "summarizes" some of the concerns of a 19th-century woman, including sewing, gardening, and religion.

W hile borders (which might be pieced, appliquéd, embroidered, fringed, or ruffled) were generally added after a quilt was completed, they seldom appear to be afterthoughts. Some borders had practical uses—to make an old quilt look newer or a small quilt bigger—but many were decorative and integral to the quilt design. In fact, the border often showed more imagination than the quilt, indicating that the quiltmaker may have reserved her most improvisational work for last.

In the Pennsylvania quilt at left, composed of some twenty-two thousand pieces, the appliqué border is actually more dominant than the quilt itself. Its wild, rambling design includes hearts, fruit, flowers, butterflies, a pair of scissors, a pocket watch, and a Bible. In the 1930s quilt above, the zigzag border complements but does not overwhelm the quilt design, which features a classic Pennsylvania tulip appliqué pattern.

The pieced border on the 1930s appliqué quilt above runs along only three of the sides. The unfinished edge was tucked out of sight under the pillows on the bed.

The highly unusual border of the 1920s Virginia quilt at right comprises woolen swatches embroidered with freeform designs. Equally imaginative is the quilt design: this personalized version of the Log Cabin pattern incorporates appliquéd animals as well as portraits of George Washington, Andrew Jackson, and Robert E. Lee into the blocks.

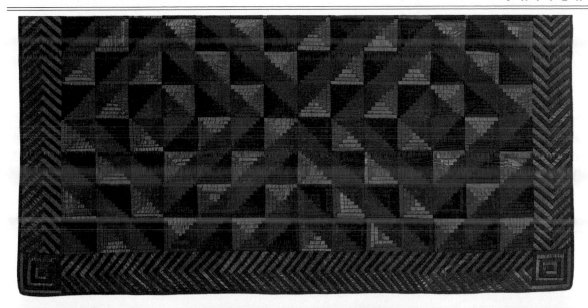

Distinctly different borders complement the three Log Cabin quilts at left. The simple chevron border on the Victorian quilt (top) was, like the rest of the quilt, sewn with silk jacket-lining scraps the maker saved from her job as a seamstress. The border on the circa 1890s child's quilt (middle) was made of scalloped silk triangles, and the circa 1865 challis crib quilt (bottom) was framed with wool tape, entwined for a ribbon-like effect.

Decorative Edging

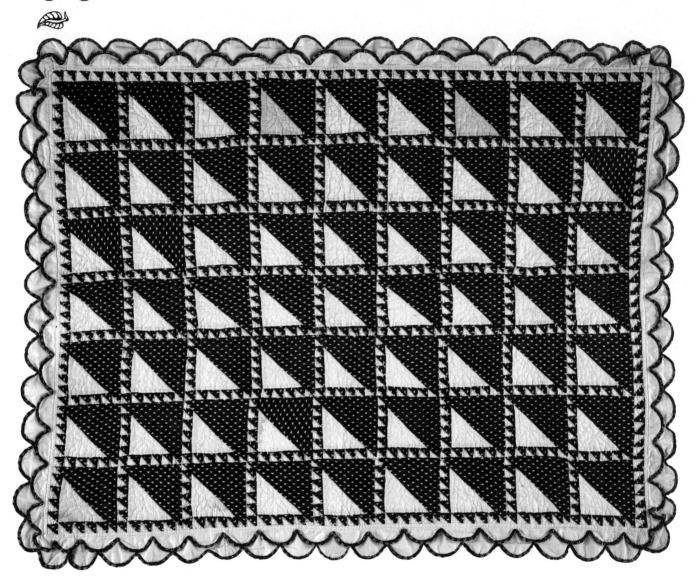

Scalloped edgings like those sewn onto the 19th-century child's quilt above were especially popular during the Victorian era.

Once a quilt is removed from the quilt frame, its edges require finishing, which is usually accomplished by adding fabric binding or by folding the backing material over the quilt top and stitching it down to create a narrow border.

Often, quiltmakers experiment, creating imaginative variations for edges, as in the late-19th-century child's quilt above. Red piping—made from the same printed cotton that was used for the quilt blocks in this Rocky Glen pattern—edges the double border of scallops.

For the 1930s Double Wedding Ring quilt opposite, the maker used a fabric "tape" and followed the contours of the appliqués, which determined the quilt's silhouette.

Black binding used for the edging picks up the black accents in the 1930s quilt opposite. The "points" in the border are formed by a continuation of the piecing design.

The Bear's Paw quilt at right
was backed with another
quilt top in similar fabrics.
Such quilts were sometimes
meant to be reversible; in
other instances the backing
might be a "failed" top that
a frugal woman hated
to waste.

Quilt Backings

While quiltmakers logically reserve their best efforts for the front of a quilt, the back of a quilt can also be appealing. Early quilt backings were often made of whatever material was on hand; it is always interesting to turn a quilt over and see what was used.

Homespun linens, including tablecloths, napkins, pillowcases, and especially sheeting, are frequently found as backings on early quilts. In times of poverty, flour, feed, and sugar sacks were cut open at the seams, washed, and sewn together for a quilt back. Other unusual backing materials included the fabric from flannel petticoats and premiums from the backs of tobacco pouches.

Once manufactured textiles became widely available at reasonable prices, during the second quarter of the 19th century, women could choose among such fabrics as calicoes, challis, and ginghams, which were known as wash goods because they laundered well.

Store-bought yardage made it easier to create a backing from one or two large pieces of fabric; this simple approach was preferred for quilt backing because there were no extra seams to quilt through. If necessary, however, the quiltmaker could also join remnants together until she had a backing that was the proper size for the quilt top. In some rare instances, a quilt might even be made with a backing that had been pieced into an actual design.

Quilt backs were commonly made from whatever materials were at hand. A plain gingham check backs the 1890s Pennsylvania Bow Tie quilt above left. The other two quilts above were made by the Mennonites in the 1880s. While Mennonite custom limits the use of printed fabrics on quilt tops to dark colors, bright prints are found on quilt backs.

At Home with Quilts

how to buy, display, and
enjoy your quilts

I t is hard not to like a quilt. Each one tells a different story, speaking of memories and family, hardships and happiness, hopes and accomplishments. And almost anyone who owns a quilt finds special pleasure in displaying it.

As you will see in this chapter, whether a quilt is used in a traditional bedroom setting, draped casually over the back of a living room sofa, or mounted as a work of art on a dining room wall, it can be an effective part of a country decor. As a colorful accessory, a quilt can set a mood, provide an unexpected accent, or become the centerpiece of a room.

It is important to remember, however, that the needlework and fabric in an old quilt are fragile, and that such a piece deserves the gentle handling that will preserve it. To that end, this chapter provides advice on buying, repairing, cleaning, and storing quilts, as well as two safe and simple methods for displaying them on walls. Properly cared for, a quilt should bring you a lifetime of enjoyment.

Two different pieced quilts bring warmth and color to a country bedroom.

Evoking Childhood

Colorful and friendly, the familiar quilt patterns shown here evoke a nostalgia for childhood. The Schoolhouse pattern, displayed by the two quilts in the New Hampshire bedroom at left, has been popular since the mid-1800s, when one-room schoolhouses were prevalent. In fact, the quilt at the foot of the bed dates from that period. Made around 1930, the crib quilt on the wall has a sawtooth border that enhances its youthful appeal.

The Alphabet pattern, above, is another longtime favorite. It was often worked by children, and afforded them the opportunity to learn needleworking and their ABCs at the same time.

Typically made by children, Alphabet quilts, like the one above, frequently display a date: because twenty-six letters cannot be divided suitably into even rows, the needleworker might add the year to fill in the leftover blocks.

Quilts in the Schoolhouse pattern add to the charm of the child's room at left.

A Vintage Frame

The quilt in progress, above, displays the Double Wedding Ring pattern. Because the circles are actually made up of many small, wedge-shaped pieces that must be joined with particular care, this is a difficult pattern to make.

The professional quiltmaker who lives in this New York City apartment often leaves her quilt frame set up in the living room while a large quilting project is in progress. Although she also works on modern frames designed for use in small spaces, she particularly likes this turn-of-the-century piece for its beautiful craftsmanship. Indeed, its worn wood and graceful lines are perfectly compatible with the other furnishings in the room, including a tall clock made around 1825 and an antique Windsor armchair. The quilt frame can be taken apart easily and stored when not in use.

The circa 1900 Mennonite quilt frame at right looks at home in a contemporary city apartment.

CLEANING A QUILT

There is one cardinal rule for cleaning a quilt: do only what you must. Cleaning is hard on most quilts, so it is necessary to weigh the risk of damaging a piece against the risk of allowing it to deteriorate by leaving it soiled.

Of all the possibilities, airing is the least dangerous, and often suffices to freshen a quilt and remove light soil. You can air a quilt indoors by laying it flat on the floor for a few hours on a blanket or sheet. If it is sturdy, you can also hang it outside on a line, but choose a dry day that is not sunny or windy. For new quilts, a gentle airing in a dryer set on a cool cycle is also acceptable.

Careful vacuuming is another way to remove dust and dirt with minimal risk. Lay the quilt on a floor or table and place fiberglass, not metal, screening over it (or cover your vacuum cleaner brush attachment with cheesecloth). With the vacuum on its lowest setting, gently run the brush over the quilt.

If you feel your quilt needs a more thorough cleaning, you will need to choose between washing and dry-cleaning. Washing is the best method for cleaning cotton and linen quilts that are colorfast and in good condition. Use a neutral detergent with no brightener or bleach (there are brands available specifically for quilts). Pretest for colorfastness by placing a few drops of water on each fabric in the quilt. Dab with a white cloth or a piece of white blotting paper (do not use paper towels; they contain acid). If the fabrics don't bleed, test again with detergent. If the fabrics still don't bleed, it is safe to wash the quilt.

Since quilts should be washed flat, you should use a large container, such as a child's wading pool. If a bathtub is your only choice, fold the quilt no more than is needed to fit.

Wash the quilt in lukewarm water following the detergent manufacturer's directions. Submerge the quilt and work it gently with your hands until the soil is removed: do not scrub, squeeze, or beat the fabric. Rinse thoroughly by draining and refilling the container or tub a few times. After the final draining, lift the quilt out very carefully—wet textiles are surprisingly heavy and can tear easily—and gently press out any excess water. Spread the quilt flat on a plastic sheet that is covered by clean towels or mattress pads, and blot gently with a dry towel. Leave the quilt undisturbed to dry. Do not iron.

Cotton or linen quilts that are not colorfast, and quilts made of silk, velvet, or wool, must be dry-cleaned. Some dry-cleaning solvents can harm quilts, so it is a good idea to contact a dealer or a museum curator who might be able to help you find a dry-cleaner equipped to work on large, fragile textiles.

The quilts at left have been set out for airing on a backyard fence. Airing outdoors should be done on a gray day: bright sunshine can cause fading.

Storing a Quilt

When quilts are not on display they should be properly stored so that they are protected from dampness, light, and dirt.

Dampness, which can lead to mildew, mold, and rot, is the single greatest enemy of quilts. Choose a well-ventilated room that is not subject to sharp variations in temperature and humidity; and keep your quilts away from direct sunshine and other bright light, which will fade and weaken the fabric fibers.

Stored quilts need protection from moths, but should not come into contact with the chemicals in mothballs. A safe alternative is an herb called southernwood (*Artemisia abrotanum*), available in dried form at home fragrance shops. Simply place some sprigs in the quilt storage area.

Quilts should also be kept away from direct contact with wood, cardboard, and paper, all of which contain acids that are damaging to fabrics. Instead, you should store them in acid-free boxes; or if you place them directly on shelves without boxes, be sure the shelf surface is coated with polyurethane or lined with acid-free tissue paper. Both acid-free boxes and acid-free tissue are available by mail order from quilting supply companies. (Never store your quilts in plastic bags; textiles need some exposure to air or they may rot.)

There are two generally accepted methods for preparing quilts for storage: rolling and folding. To roll a quilt, use a large cardboard or plastic tube—4½ inches or more in diameter—covered with acid-free tissue paper or a prewashed fabric such as muslin or cotton-polyester sheeting. The tube can be hung on brackets or from chains, or laid on a shelf. (Although rolling helps prevent creasing, some experts recommend it only for thin quilts, quilt tops, or coverlets.)

Folding is the best method for storing a multilayered quilt because it is less stressful on the various layers than rolling, and it is less apt to cause buckling. The quilt, however, should be folded as few times as possible. In the method shown at right, the quilt is laid flat, top up, and lined with one layer of acid-free tissue. It is then folded in thirds, and then folded in thirds again. Each fold is padded with loosely rolled acid-free tissue to prevent creasing.

After the quilt is folded, it should be wrapped in muslin or a clean sheet and stored in an acid-free box or on a protected shelf. To prevent the quilt from wearing or discoloring at the folds, take it out every two or three months and carefully refold it with the tissue rolls placed in slightly different positions.

The proper method for folding quilts for storage, right, involves lining the quilt and padding the folds with acid-free tissue paper. The quilt is then ready to be stored in an acid-free box.

A. Lay quilt flat, top up; line with acid-free tissue. Place loose roll of tissue one third of way down for first fold.

B. Fold upper third of quilt down over roll. Place second roll of tissue one third up from bottom for second fold.

C. Fold lower third of quilt up over roll, aligning edge with first fold. Smooth out wrinkles.

D. Place third roll of tissue one third in from left end of quilt. Fold left side of quilt over tissue.

E. Place fourth roll of tissue across center of folded quilt so that right side can be folded toward center.

F. Fold right side of quilt over roll. Quilt is now ready to be stored following directions opposite.

A Rustic Look

Displaying a pattern particularly popular in the 1850s, the Log Cabin quilt above picks up the rustic theme of this room, and blends well with the mottled colors of the hooked rug on the wall.

The colorful patterns of quilts can be used effectively to enhance a room's decor. In the Texas bedroom at right and above—designed for a child who loves horses—two striking quilts help set a rustic theme and complement a collection of folk art.

The quilt on the bed displays the Princess Feather pattern, which originated in the eastern colonies but traveled west with settlers in the mid-1800s. The design blends with the feathery motif in the crewel-embroidered curtains. The Log Cabin quilt above, worked in simple calicoes, is another subtle reference to frontier life.

The Princess Feather pattern in the 1800s quilt at right was a favorite during frontier days.

Unexpected Accents

*Covered by a Diagonal
Triangles quilt, the 19th-
century hired-hand's bed in
the hallway at right is an
imaginative alternative to
traditional seating. The
cheery colors of the quilt
brighten the wood-paneled
hall and blend with the
handmade chenille rug
hanging beside
the door.*

Shown off in an entryway or hallway, a quilt can provide a surprising and welcome design accent. The owner of the rustic house at left, for example, added color to her front entry by displaying a Diagonal Triangles quilt on the 19th-century hired-hand's bed she keeps there. (Such beds, which were originally placed in attics, were built low to the floor to fit under the sloping ceiling.) The simple quilt pattern suits the primitive look of the bed, creat-

ing an unusual focal point in the small space.

The owner of the two quilts above has more than one hundred in her collection, and takes pleasure in displaying them throughout her Pennsylvania home. In an upstairs hall, shown here, she exhibits a Diagonal Triangles quilt by simply draping it over a blanket chest. On the chest, a tiny twig doll bed—a contemporary folk-art piece—is covered with a miniature quilt pieced from antique fabrics.

Displayed on a blanket chest, the Diagonal Triangles quilt above becomes a handsome accessory,

picking up the colors in the Staffordshire china on the shelves. A doll quilt covers the tiny twig bed.

CRIB AND DOLL QUILTS

Whether stitched by an expert needleworker or made by a child just learning to sew, vintage crib and doll quilts have particular appeal as diminutive labors of love.

Crib and doll quilts are not just small, they are actually scaled-down versions of full-size quilts: the blocks, borders, and individual motifs are all miniaturized. The care that was lavished on planning and executing these small designs adds to their charm as well as to their value.

In general, crib quilts show a greater range in design than doll quilts. There are essentially two types of crib quilts: simple pieced examples made for everyday use, and elaborate quilts that were intended as heirlooms. The fancier crib quilts, popular throughout the 1800s, reflect the major traditions in 19th-century quilt design, including whitework and *broderie perse,* pieced and appliquéd block patterns, and even crazy patchworks. Beautifully stitched, many were designed by young women to match the wedding quilts in their trousseaux; others were made for christenings.

Beginning in the early 20th century, crib quilts were more often apt to be appliquéd or embroidered with motifs such as animals, which were appealing to children. During the 1930s, the trend toward pastels for quilts prompted the color schemes of pink for girls and blue for boys.

While crib quilts are generally only a yard square, doll quilts are even tinier—sometimes as small as twelve inches square. Some doll quilts were sewn by children: their small size made it easy for a little girl to learn how to plan a design, cut the pieces, and practice her stitches while at the same time producing something special for her doll. Often the piecing stitches appear far more tentative than the quilting stitches. It is clear that in these instances the quilt tops were given to a more experienced needleworker, who completed the quilting. Even though doll quilts received hard use as playthings, some examples— probably made by adults as gifts for children—display extraordinarily intricate designs and fine quilting.

Care should be taken when purchasing doll and crib quilts: many have been faked by cutting down old full-size quilts or quilt tops. You will find that such examples are usually not scaled properly, nor do they show telltale wear and fading around the edges. And look out for freshly applied binding; even if it is made from old fabric, it is hard to disguise, and its stitching will look new.

Doll quilts were often made by children learning to sew, crib quilts by indulgent grandmothers. Today, such diminutive quilts, like those at left, are treasured by collectors.

Period Patterns

The pastel colors in the 1930s Grandmother's Flower Garden quilt used to upholster the chair and hassock above are typical of many Depression-era quilts.

The patterns and colors of Depression-era quilts work well in these two country rooms. In the feminine bedroom sitting area above, a 1930s quilt in the Grandmother's Flower Garden pattern—especially popular in the first decades of the 20th century—was reused as upholstery for an easy chair and hassock. A quilt in the same pattern but in different colors makes a complementary throw. In the bedroom at right, a heart-appliqué quilt, made in the late 1920s, blends easily with 18th-century furniture and a hooked rug.

In the Texas bedroom at right, a 1920s quilt covers a country Sheraton field bed.

Handsome Backdrops

The colors and geometric designs in Log Cabin quilts can produce interesting optical effects that are shown off to advantage when such a quilt is displayed on a wall. The design of the Log Cabin crib quilt over the mantel at right gives it a three-dimensional look that makes the quilt seem larger than it is.

Whether small or large, a well-displayed quilt not only can stand on its own as a decoration, but it can also become an effective backdrop for other furnishings.

Mounted over the mantel in the Maryland living room at left, a tiny crib quilt—made in the Log Cabin pattern—appropriately sets off the owner's collection of early-20th-century log-cabin toys. Its color scheme and geometric design also complement the room's primitive furniture.

In the New York City living room above, a silk-and-wool Log Cabin quilt silhouetted against a white wall unifies the studied composition of country furnishings.

Distinguished by delicate silk and wool fabrics as well as fine featherstitching, the Log Cabin quilt above not only sets off a simple furniture arrangement, but is a work of art in itself.

DISPLAYING A QUILT

If you own a quilt, it is only natural to want to display it. What fun is it to keep a beautiful work of art in a dark closet? It is important, however, to take particular care to protect a valuable, vulnerable textile while showing it off.

The directions opposite describe two reliable methods for hanging quilts. In one, a dowel rod or lattice strip is placed in a muslin sleeve sewn onto the back side of the quilt. In the other method, Velcro tape is sewn onto the back side of the quilt and affixed to a lattice strip that has been mounted on the wall.

Only quilts that are sturdy and not too heavy should be hung in either manner. Ideally, more than one edge of the quilt should be prepared for hanging, so that you can periodically turn the quilt to redistribute the weight. It is best to alternate a quilt between storage and display about every six months.

If you do not want to hang a quilt, there are other possibilities for display, but remember the following: any quilt should be displayed away from direct sunlight and bright artificial light. If you are draping a quilt over a wooden table, rack, or chair, be sure to protect it from acids in the wood by first covering the furniture with a piece of muslin or acid-free tissue. Redrape or refold the quilt frequently. Even displayed on a bed, a quilt can sag, so it is a good idea to remove it occasionally to relieve it from stress.

MUSLIN SLEEVE

VELCRO STRIP

◆ MATERIALS

Preshrunk medium-weight muslin, white or colorfast (see directions for amount) · 1-inch dowel rod or 1⅛ inch-wide (or wider) lattice strip, 2 inches longer than hanging edge of quilt · Sandpaper

◆ DIRECTIONS

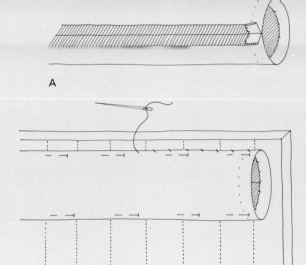

A

1. Lay quilt flat with back side up. To make sleeve, cut strip of muslin 7 inches wide and 2 inches longer than hanging edge of quilt.

2. Turn up 1½ inches at each end of strip, then hem.

3. Fold strip in half lengthwise with wrong sides together; machine-stitch ½-inch seam along long edge. Open seam and center it on sleeve (Illustration A), then iron seam and sleeve flat.

4. With seam side down, lay sleeve on quilt ½ inch in from hanging edge, centering sleeve between ends; there should be ½ inch of quilt showing beyond each end of sleeve. (Even if hanging edge of quilt is not straight, lay sleeve straight, or quilt will ripple or sag when hung.) Pin sleeve; slipstitch to quilt along long edges and quilt-side of sleeve ends, keeping sleeve open (Illustration B), and sewing through all layers of quilt using small, unobtrusive stitches. Remove pins.

5. If necessary, smooth dowel or lattice strip with sandpaper; slide through sleeve, and attach to the wall as desired.

B

◆ MATERIALS

Preshrunk medium-weight muslin, white or colorfast (see directions for amount) · 1⅛-inch wide lattice strip, same length as hanging edge of quilt · 1-inch wide Velcro tape, same length as hanging edge of quilt · Velcro adhesive · Sandpaper

◆ DIRECTIONS

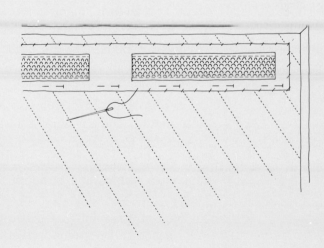

1. Cut strip of muslin 3 inches wide and 2 inches longer than hanging edge of quilt. Separate the Velcro tape. Cut loop tape into 6-inch pieces.

2. Turn under 1½ inches at each end of muslin strip, then hem. Center loop pieces on strip, placing pieces about 2 inches apart and so that they are ¾ inch from ends of strip. Machine-stitch pieces of tape to muslin along long edges. Turn under ½ inch along long edges of strip; iron.

3. Lay quilt flat with back side up. Pin muslin strip to hanging edge of quilt as in Step 4 of directions above. Slipstitch to quilt on all sides (see illustration); remove pins.

4. If necessary, smooth lattice strip with sandpaper. Attach hook tape to lattice strip, using Velcro adhesive.

5. Fasten lattice strip to wall, as desired. Press loop tape on quilt top to hook tape on lattice strip until quilt is held firmly in position.

A Unified Mix

Occasionally, when a quilt wore out it was saved and reused as the lining for a new quilt. Made at the beginning of the 20th century, the appliqué quilt above encloses an appliqué quilt from the 1800s. When held up to the light, the patterns of both quilt tops can be seen.

E ven when it has a distinctive look of its own, a quilt can mix well with other tex-tiles in a room. In the bedroom at right, the homeowner has effectively combined an early-20th-century appliqué quilt with a mid-1800s coverlet on the bed; the chaise is covered with Federal-style upholstery and the carpet is an early-1900s Heriz. While the textiles are from different periods, they are unified by a tradi-tional feeling and a predominance of red.

The homeowner takes particular pride in the quilt, distinguished by unusual heart and oak leaf motifs. The asymmetrical shapes have a whimsical, freeform look even though they were cut with a template, and the arrangement of the appliqués, which at first appears random, ac-tually forms a carefully planned repeat pattern.

Yet even more intriguing than the quilt's de-sign is the fact that the top and backing encase an 1800s quilt. The appliqué in the older quilt top can be seen when the quilt is held up to the light, as above. Curiously, the two quilt tops were made with nearly identical red calicoes.

Although it was made in the 1930s, the quilt displayed on the bed at left is still compatible with the early American feeling of this bedroom, where a variety of textiles produces a rich combination of textures and colors.

BUYING A QUILT: WHAT TO LOOK FOR

Perhaps the most important thing you can do as a potential quilt buyer is invest your time before you invest your money. Many considerations will affect your purchase, but above all, you should know what you like and understand what you are buying.

If you are unfamiliar with quilts, it is a good idea to begin by reading widely and looking at photographs. Visit museums so that you can spend time examining quilts of exceptional quality; and if possible, talk to curators about particular types that interest you. This will help you learn to recognize fine design, expert piecing, and skillful quilting, and it will provide you with an excellent frame of reference.

Once you are ready to buy, go to a dealer of good reputation; dealers generally work out of their own shops and also show their wares at antiques fairs. Make sure the dealer lets you examine any quilt that you are considering purchasing.

Begin by assessing the physical condition of the quilt. Look for problems that can reduce its value, such as wear, fading, color bleeding, yellowing, moth holes, rust, water stains, and mildew. Be sure to check for acid burns, which often appear on red and brown fabrics that were

dyed with iron oxides. "Boxing stains," from the acids in wooden storage containers, and "foxing"—oil stains from cotton seeds left in the batting—are other common problems in old quilts.

You will also want to check for repairs and other changes to the quilt. Are all the pieces of the quilt top made

of the original fabric? If there is a combination of older and newer fabrics, was it done when the quilt was made; if it was done later, how much later? (Old repairs do not necessarily detract from the value of a quilt, but new ones do.) Are the quilt top and back consistent in period? Was the quilting added later? (Some old tops, newly backed and quilted, are sold as

antiques.) Are the borders irregular? Has the binding been replaced? If so, the quilt may have been cut down or rebound.

If stains, damage, and recent repairs do exist, they will usually reduce the value of the quilt—but that doesn't necessarily mean the textile isn't worth purchasing. While some problems, such as fading and bleeding, are irreversible, many can be corrected by a professional conservator.

Cleaning and restoring antique quilts, however, are both controversial issues. Some experts say it is better to clean an old quilt to help prevent its deterioration than to let it remain soiled or covered with stains. Others prefer the "crispness" and patina that develops when the fabric is left alone. Many collectors, in fact, will not even consider buying quilts that have been washed or repaired.

In any case, consult an expert to determine whether the repair or restoration of a particular quilt is recommended—or possible. As a rule, it is better to do nothing than to effect a poor restoration. If repairs are undertaken, they should be done extremely carefully, using period fabrics and stitching that blend in unobtrusively with the originals. Many people prefer to purchase an old quilt and simply leave alone any damage or stains.

Before buying, you will want to consider the age of the quilt. As a very general rule, the older the quilt, the more it is worth. Ask for a written history that includes any information the dealer might know, including the

Tiny, even stitches indicate superior quilting.

names of the maker and others who have owned it. Such documentation will add to the quilt's historical interest as well as to its value. If the quilt has no documentation and is not marked by the maker, you will need to examine the fabric, pattern, con-

Small, precisely cut pieces can contribute to a quilt's value.

struction technique, and quilting to try to determine its age.

Old age is not the only determi-nant of value. Imaginative and unu-sual appliqué, piecing, and quilting patterns can also affect the price. Quilts with original designs are gen-erally more expensive than those made from kits, which first became available in the 1920s. A kit-made quilt that displays personal varia-tions in fabric or design, however, can be highly valued.

Workmanship is very important as well. Look for precise cutting and stitching in the quilt top, and check for fine quilting stitches (nine stitches or more to the inch is considered a good measure of skill). In a pieced

Acid burns caused by old dyes are irreversible.

quilt, observe the number and size of the pieces; the greater the number of pieces and the smaller their size, the more valuable the quilt. (Note, however, that some antique quilts were made with a deliberate flaw in color, stitching, or construction as an expression of the quiltmak-er's traditional belief that only God creates perfection.)

All other things being equal, ap-pliqué quilts are more expensive to-day than pieced quilts, which were more commonly made for everyday

An obvious repair will reduce the value of a quilt.

use and sometimes show inferior workmanship. Album quilts, in par-ticular, are costly because each ex-ample is unique. An early pieced quilt that shows high-quality work-manship, however, will also bring top dollar.

A good repair blends in with the original work unobtrusively.

Finally, the bottom line when buy-ing a quilt should be your own taste. If you see a quilt that particularly appeals to you, you should probably purchase it. Whatever its type, color, pattern, age, and condition—and no matter what its historical, aesthetic, or monetary value might be—you will be happier living with a quilt if you truly like it.

Creating a Mood

Yo-Yo quilts are not technically quilts but pieced coverlets that are made without a backing or batting. The solid white spread used underneath the colorful Yo-Yo quilt above and at right helps set off the individual rosettes.

Often a quilt can establish the mood of a room: the romantic feeling of this bedroom comes from a charming Yo-Yo quilt, seen at right and in detail above, displayed on a painted Victorian bed.

A Yo-Yo quilt is one of the many types of the so-called novelty quilts that were popular in the 1930s. Each "yo-yo" is made by sewing a running stitch around the edge of a small circle of fabric, then pulling the thread tight to gather the fabric into a puckered rosette that resembles half a yo-yo. The yo-yos are then sewn together, without a backing, to complete the quilt. Often made in pastels, such quilts have an appealing, feminine quality.

The pretty pastels of a Yo-Yo quilt enhance the romantic look of this bedroom.

Quilts as Art

Displaying the graphic Double Irish Chain pattern, popular in this country since the late 1750s, the quilt above is presented as a handsome wall-hanging in a New York City dining room.

Whaile America's early quiltmakers took pride in their needlework skills, few would have guessed that their quilts would one day be regarded as art.

Indeed, today quilts are probably displayed as often as they are used for bedding. Hung on the wall, the quilts in these two dining rooms, for example, take the place of paintings. The 19th-century Double Irish Chain quilt above provides a striking focal point in the room. At right, an Ocean Waves crib quilt made around 1870 is a subtle counterpoint to a quiet color scheme.

An Ocean Waves quilt provides visual interest in the pleasingly austere dining room at right.

Bold Graphics

The simple, graphic patterns and intense colors of Amish and Mennonite quilts can adapt surprisingly well to different country looks. In the cozy bedroom at left, the rich colors of the 19th-century Amish Diamond in the Square quilt on the bed blend easily with the traditional decor.

In the narrow hallway above, both the 1800s Mennonite crib quilt and the larger Amish quilt serve as "modern art," transforming the space with their bold, optically interesting designs.

A wool Amish quilt complements the traditional look of the late-18th-century Sheraton bed, left.

Hung away from direct light, a cotton Mennonite crib quilt and a larger cotton-and-wool Amish quilt, both from the 1800s, bring color to the narrow hallway above.

Quilting Projects

*a table runner, a crib quilt,
Amish pillows, and a
quilt for your bed*

Whether you are an experienced needleworker or a person who has never sewn before, making a quilt—or a smaller quilted piece—can provide pleasant rewards. There is a special satisfaction derived from picking a pattern and fabrics that please you, making templates, cutting the fabric pieces, and finally doing the actual quilting itself. These steps may seem complicated, but as this chapter shows, there are actually very few techniques and stitches to master.

The projects that follow range from a pieced table runner to an appliqué bed quilt, progressing from simple quiltmaking techniques to more complex methods. All except the bed quilt can be made entirely on the sewing machine. The ideas on these pages should serve as a starting point. When you learn more about quilting, you will want to create patterns and designs of your own. Include family and friends in the process; much of the fun of quiltmaking comes from sharing the experience with others.

The varied sewing supplies used in a quilt project range from pins to templates.

General Directions

Unlike dressmaking, which involves a number of elaborate sewing techniques, quiltmaking requires the mastery of only one or two simple stitches and some slight knowledge of fabrics, pinning, and assembly. The equipment required is also minimal: you don't even need a sewing machine.

These general directions include the basic information necessary to make the four projects that follow. It is suggested that you read through this section before undertaking any of the projects. Then, when the directions for a specific project refer you back to these pages, you will be familiar with the material.

It is also suggested that you consult the staff of a quilting supply shop or a fabric store if you need help in selecting the correct equipment or fabrics for these projects.

EQUIPMENT

The basic supplies needed for making a quilt can be kept in a medium-size sewing basket. They include scissors, pins, needles, thread, a thimble, and a ruler. Such items, however, can vary greatly in quality. If you are planning to make more than one of these projects—or to pursue quilting seriously—you should buy the best available equipment at the outset.

Scissors are the most expensive item you will need for most small quilting projects. A good pair should last a lifetime if you do not misuse them. For cutting fabric, many people, especially those who already know dressmaking, prefer shears (large scissors) with a bent handle

(Illustration A). Such shears come in several lengths, and the size you choose will depend on the size of

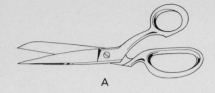

A

your hand and how the shears feel when you use them. For left-handers, models are available through sewing or quilting supply stores, usually by special order. If you do use dressmaker's shears for cutting fabric, you will also need a pair of small embroidery scissors, such as the ones in the shape of a stork (Illustration B), for snipping thread, clipping curves, and trimming corners.

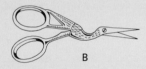

B

In general, small scissors, about 6 inches overall, with straight blades and two round finger grips, are fine for all quilting purposes. A new type, called appliqué scissors (Illustration C), has a wide flange on one blade to aid in cutting smoothly through delicate fabrics and around tiny curves.

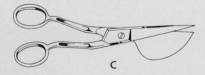

C

Two types of straight pins are needed for quilting. For piecing, they should be fine and sharp. The best ones are called silk pins. For pinning the layers of a quilt together prior to quilting, larger pins with round

heads, called quilter's pins, are used. These should also be of the best quality, so that the points stay sharp and do not damage fabrics.

Needles should be short and as fine as possible (the slimmer the better). The larger the needle number, the finer the needle and the smaller the eye. The choice of most quilters is a type called "betweens" in sizes 8, 9, or 10. Some very expert quilters pride themselves on using a size 12. Betweens come in mixed-size packs, so you can experiment until you find a size you like.

There are many types of thread available. A fine, good-quality all-cotton thread, in neutral or in the colors of your quilt pieces, is usually easiest to use.

While some people find using a thimble irritating, a thimble is almost essential in quilting. Most quilting teachers suggest that you buy one of durable silver that fits the middle finger of your sewing hand, and wear it every time you sew.

Other materials include a sharp lead pencil, which is needed to trace pattern pieces and quilting designs onto the fabric. A 60-inch tape measure is helpful for checking the widths of fabrics and the lengths of long sashes and borders. It is also convenient to have a small 6-inch ruler with a slide that can be set for checking pieced sections, blocks, and sashes to make sure they are exactly the same size.

You will need an iron and ironing board, if only small ones, in the room where you work; every seam in a quilt has to be ironed after it is stitched.

Finally, to make the Vase of Tulips quilt (page 162), you will also need a quilting frame (see Quilting Frames, pages 148-149).

FABRIC AND
ITS TREATMENT

The fabric you select for these and most quilting projects will probably be cotton or a cotton blend, both of which generally come in 45-inch widths. Once you have chosen your quilt design, you can usually figure the yardage required on the basis of 45-inch fabric.

All woven fabric has two straight-grain, or thread, lines: the lengthwise grain runs parallel to the selvage edges, and the cross grain runs perpendicular to the selvages. Before working with the fabric, check to see that the two grains are straight and at right angles to each other. If they are not, pull the short corners of the fabric on the bias to align the grains.

Two other potential problems with cotton fabric are shrinkage and fading or running of colors. For suggestions on coping with these problems, see Choosing Quilt Fabrics, pages 100-101.

MAKING TEMPLATES

Templates, or the pattern pieces used for piecing, appliqué, and quilting, are available in quilting supply stores in many sizes, shapes, and materials. Many quiltmakers prefer to make their own templates, however, especially when working from patterns like the ones in this book. For making your own templates, some additional equipment is needed.

The material for the template itself can be anything from a good grade of shirt cardboard to a hard (usually translucent) stencil plastic, available at quilting supply shops and art supply stores. While these materials can be cut with good paper shears, a stencil knife, available at art supply and stationery stores, is preferable. If you do use a stencil knife, a narrow straightedge, 12 or more inches long and preferably made of metal, will aid in cutting.

The first step in making templates from patterns in a book or magazine is to trace all the pattern pieces along the seam lines onto a sheet of tissue or lightweight typing paper.

Patterns for appliqué templates are cut along the outline of the pieces, which are then traced onto the template material.

Patterns for piecing templates are traced to form a full-size version of the scaled piecing diagram. This helps you check whether the printing of the pattern pieces has caused any small inaccuracies. If inaccuracies do exist, they should be corrected by careful remeasuring and redrawing of lines and angles. You can then cut and trace the pieces onto the template material.

Making templates for pieced patterns can be done in one of two ways. Pieced-quilt pieces almost always have a seam allowance of ¼ inch. If you intend to piece by hand, your template should be cut out along the seam line (the inner, broken line on the pattern piece). You will add the ¼-inch seam allowance by eye when you cut out the fabric pieces (Illustration D-1).

If you plan to piece by machine, it is often easier to use a pattern for each template that is cut out along the

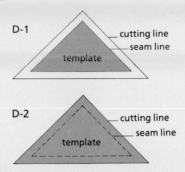

cutting line of the piece (Illustration D-2) and then traced onto the template material. When you stitch, your seam allowance guideline will be the ¼-inch mark on the faceplate of the sewing machine.

MARKING AND CUTTING
THE FABRIC

To mark the pieces for cutting, lay the fabric wrong side up on a flat surface. Weight the fabric at the corners to keep it flat. Check the lengthwise grain against the suggested grain line marked on the pattern pieces; the grains should be parallel. Occasionally, you may want to lay pieces on the cross grain in order to arrange stripes or to vary patterns. Whichever way you work, if you are using templates that were cut on the seam line, you must remember to leave ½ inch between pieces for the ¼-inch seam allowance. On the wrong side of the fabric, trace around the template with a sharp pencil.

With sharp scissors, cut carefully either on the pencil line or ¼ inch beyond it, depending on the type of template you are using. Stack the pieces in "same kind" piles.

PINNING AND SEWING

Careful pinning is adequate preparation for piecing; no basting is required. (For information on how to handle appliqué pieces, see page 166.) Use only fine silk pins for this purpose; the large heads of quilter's pins can damage your sewing machine, or get in the way when you are piecing by hand. Place the pieces with right sides together, raw edges even, and pin directly on the seam line, or ¼ inch from the edge, picking up as little of both layers of fabric as possible and placing the pins at right angles to the seam line. Start pinning at each end and then fill in between as necessary (Illustration E).

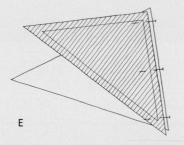

E

A number of patterns, like the Wild Goose Chase (page 151) and the Little Schoolhouse (page 159), fall easily into piecing units. Pin the pieces together into as many of these units as is convenient at one time; then stitch and iron them.

For each seam, you will use a running stitch secured at either end by a backstitch. To do this, tie a small, neat knot in the end of the thread. Start by pushing the needle down through the fabric at the starting point of the seam line. Then backstitch by bringing it up a little farther along the line and putting it back down and up again at the same points.

Then proceed along the seam line with a running, or in-and-out, stitch, and finish off the seam with a double backstitch (Illustration F).

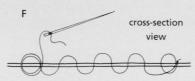

F   cross-section view

When machine-stitching seams, be sure that the machine tension is even, and that the stitch gauge is set for no fewer than 10 or 12 stitches to the inch. There will be no need to backstitch or tie off thread at the ends. Stitch from one raw edge directly along the seam line and off the other raw edge.

IRONING

It is absolutely necessary to iron as you go along: each seam in a quilt should be ironed before another seam is stitched across it. In quiltmaking, seams are usually ironed to one side. If possible, iron the seam toward the darker of the two fabrics, so that the dark seam allowances do not show through the lighter fabric. If this is not possible, be sure to trim off any dark edges of the seam allowance that might show.

BATTING, BACKING, TYING, AND QUILTING

Most quilts have three layers: top, batting, and backing. Quilt batting is made from various materials—cotton, polyester, wool, silk, and blends—and comes in different thicknesses. In general, a thinner batting is easier to handle and allows the quilting to show up more.

Fabric used to back a quilt may be

pieced crosswise or lengthwise—using as few seams as possible—so that it is a little larger than the top. Be sure to cut off the selvages, which can shrink and ruin the quilt.

If no batting is used, the quilt is generally referred to as a coverlet, and is tied in order to hold the top and backing together. Tying, in fact, is a fast way to secure the layers on any quilt. It is recommended for quilts with very thick batting or with tops that do not always lend themselves to quilting, such as crazy quilts. Many smaller projects, such as wall hangings and table runners, are also finished in this way.

To attach the backing and batting to a quilt top before tying, follow the directions given in Quilting Frames (pages 148-149), then decide where you want the ties to fall: most quilters place them at the corners or centers of blocks, or at measured intervals across the surface. Working with yarn or embroidery thread, push the needle down through all the layers of the quilt from the top, leaving a few inches of yarn or thread sticking out. Bring the needle back up about ⅛ inch away. Take one more stitch in exactly the same place as the first. You will now have two ends and a small stitch on the top of the fabric. Tie the ends in a square knot, cut them to about ¾ inch, and leave them as a decoration (Illustration G).

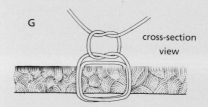

G   cross-section view

To prepare a top for quilting, mark the quilt design, using a template, stencil, or yardstick—depending on the design chosen—and a sharp lead pencil (or dressmaker's chalk for dark fabric). For crosshatch quilting, you may use the narrow masking tape made especially for this purpose, which eliminates marking. Many appliqué designs, including the Vase of Tulips (page 162), are enhanced by quilting an outline around the appliqué pieces, then filling in the background with a straight-line or crosshatch pattern (Illustration H).

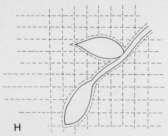

H

For instructions on how to attach the quilt layers to a frame to ready them for quilting, see Quilting Frames, pages 148-149.

The quilting stitch used by most quilters is the same small running stitch used in joining seams by hand. Decide whether you wish to start quilting at the center of the quilt or at a border. Practice will make your stitches smaller, neater, and straighter. There are no absolute rules for quilt stitchery, so you can gradually develop your own style.

BINDING

Whether a quilt is made with or without batting, the edges are generally bound in fabric. The directions that follow are for one type of binding—a single-layer bias

binding. It is probably the easiest to handle and can be made from any fabric.

To make a bias binding, pick a fabric that matches or complements your quilt, and be sure that the fabric grains are straight. Cut one end along the cross grain. Fold the fabric so that the cross grain lies directly on the lengthwise grain. Crease along the bias line, unfold, and mark the bias line, using a pencil and yardstick.

A ³⁄₈-inch binding is an appropriate width for most quilts. The width of the fabric you cut should be slightly more than four times the desired finished width, or 1⅝ inches for a ³⁄₈-inch binding. Using a pencil and yardstick, draw lines 1⅝ inches apart, parallel to the bias line, and cut the number of strips necessary to make the required binding length. Piece the ends by placing the right sides together at right angles and stitching a ¼-inch seam. (Illustration I). Iron the seams open.

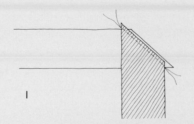

I

Lay the quilt flat, and measure across the center, top to bottom and side to side. Trim the edges even, and baste the layers together around the edges, holding in any fullness to the measurements you just made. This will prevent the edges of the finished quilt from rippling after it is bound.

Start at the center of one side of the quilt top and, with the right sides

together, lay the binding along the raw edge of the quilt, pinning a scant ³⁄₈ inch in from the raw edge. Stitch the binding to the quilt edge, leaving a ³⁄₈-inch seam allowance.

Either trim all corners to a gentle curve—to make them easier to bind around—or make a small miter pleat at each corner to ease the fabric. To miter, end the stitching ³⁄₈ inch from the upcoming corner and backstitch to finish (Illustration J-1). Fold a

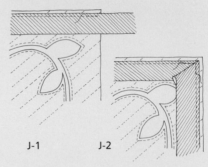

J-1   J-2

small pleat into the binding at the corner, then start stitching again ³⁄₈ inch along on the next side (Illustration J-2). Continue in this manner all the way around the quilt. Cut off the end of the binding, leaving a small overlap, which will be folded under to cover the raw end where the binding began.

Fold the binding over the edge of the quilt to the back. Fold under ¼ inch at the raw edge, and pin along the stitching line (Illustration K). Blind-stitch the folded edge against the stitching line.

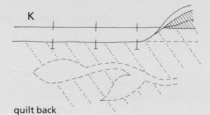

K

quilt back

QUILTING FRAMES

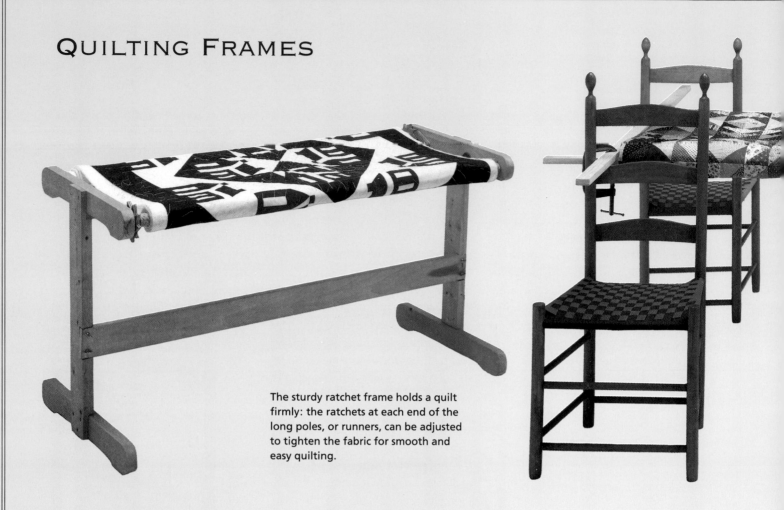

The sturdy ratchet frame holds a quilt firmly: the ratchets at each end of the long poles, or runners, can be adjusted to tighten the fabric for smooth and easy quilting.

Once a quilt top is pieced or appliquéd, it is generally layered with batting, or filler, and a backing of cloth, and then all three layers are stitched together. This stitching process—the actual *quilting*—is an important step in creating a beautiful quilt. Whether your quilting is elaborate or simple, you will need to attach the layers to a frame and stretch them to keep them from shifting or bunching while you stitch.

Quilting frames have not changed much over the years, but it is no longer necessary to build one: today the ratchet frame (above left) and the hoop frame (far right, above) are available from quilting supply stores.

A simple and versatile frame, however, can easily be put together at home, using four 2- x 1-inch pieces of lumber, four C-clamps, and four ladder-back chairs. This so-called four-stout-sticks frame (above center) is particularly convenient because the frame can simply be taken off the chairs and leaned against a wall when no one is quilting. Like the more elaborate ratchet frame, the stout-sticks frame also allows a quilter to roll the quilt.

The lengths of wood needed for a stout-sticks frame will vary according to the size of your quilt, but most important is that the longer pieces, called runners, accommodate the widest dimension of the quilt. The length of the stationary pieces, or stretchers, can be adjusted to ex-

pose as much of the quilt as desired.

Whether you use a stout-sticks frame or a ratchet frame, you will need to wrap the runners with a sturdy fabric, such as muslin, so that the quilt can be attached with pins and rolled without damaging the fabrics. For this you will need two muslin strips about 4 to 6 inches wide and as long as the runners. Fold the strips in half lengthwise and staple them to the runners.

To ready the quilt layers for the frame, first lay the backing right side down, smooth and square, in a large, clear floor space. Lay the batting on the backing, smoothing any wrinkles with your hands and being careful not to stretch the batting. Lay the finished top (already marked with the quilting

The "four-stout-sticks" frame has been used by quilters for generations. Made with 2- x 1-inch lumber, C-clamps, and ladder-back chairs, it can be adjusted in size according to the number of quilters who will be working at it.

A hoop frame works exactly like a large embroidery hoop and is useful for both small and large quilting projects. Available in diameters of 18 to 24 inches, hoop frames can be held on the lap or mounted on a stand. Never leave your work in a hoop for any length of time, since it can permanently mark the fabric.

pattern) wrong side down on the batting, checking to see that all the pieces are square. Then, using large quilter's pins, pin through the layers in radiating lines from the center to the corners and sides, continuing to check that the layers are still square.

You will then need to baste the layers together. You can baste along the pin lines while the quilt is still on the floor, or you can stretch the quilt on one of the large frames and then baste. This is easier to do with the stout-sticks frame than with the ratchet frame, since once you have pinned the quilt to the runners of the stout-sticks frame, you can simply stretch it out flat and adjust the clamps to give it the proper tension. With the ratchet frame, you must roll one edge of the quilt with the pins in it, and this requires some care.

Once the quilt is basted, roll it to a convenient width for quilting—usually as far as you can comfortably reach, or so that it is wide enough for quilters to work on both sides. You may want to pin some 1-inch-wide strips of muslin or woven tape to the raw sides of the quilt and then tie them to the stretcher. This will aid in keeping the quilt taut.

If a large frame is inconvenient, the hoop frame, which holds the fabric taut between an inner ring and an outer one, is a good alternative. Ideal for small quilting projects, the hoop frame is also useful for quilting larger pieces that have already been stretched and basted.

WILD GOOSE CHASE TABLE RUNNER

A table runner can be an attractive alternative to a tablecloth in a country dining room. Making one will give you an opportunity to display your patchwork virtuosity. The Wild Goose Chase pattern shown here originated in the early 19th century, and is just one of many Flying Geese patterns popular today. In this version, rows of triangles pieced in random color combinations are arranged in alternating directions. The darker triangles represent geese flying.

Repetitive pieced designs like this one were often planned as a way to use up sewing scraps. It is surprising the number of colors that look good together against the right neutral background fabrics. You can buy fabrics or choose them from your scrap bag. You might want to make runners in different color combinations, for a seasonal change.

The pattern can, of course, be lengthened or shortened to fit your table. When buying fabric, you will have to increase or decrease the yardages accordingly. You can also adapt the pattern to make a full-size bed quilt by simply increasing the number and length of the pieced strips, and by batting, backing, and tying the quilt following the instructions given in the General Directions, pages 144-147.

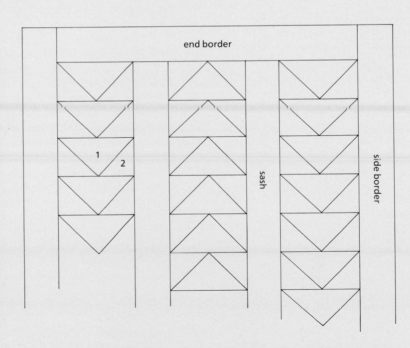

Scaled piecing diagram   Shown here in reduction is the exact arrangement of the pieces in the table runner at left.

ASSEMBLY

The finished runner is 65 x 20½ inches, including binding. No batting is used. See the General Directions, pages 144-147, for suggested sewing equipment, notes on fabric, and instructions for making and using pattern templates, pinning and cutting fabric, piecing by hand or by machine, and making bias binding.

1. With right sides together, pin long edges of two #2 pieces to short edges of each #1 piece. Stitch ¼-inch seams, remove pins, and iron seams toward #2 pieces. You will now have a small rectangle made up of one #1 and two #2 pieces (Illustration A).

2. When you have made 90 such rectangles, arrange them in three rows of 30 rectangles each, so that the juxtapositions of colors please you. With right sides together, pin and stitch rectangles together into three strips. Remove pins, and iron seams toward #1 pieces (Illustration B).

3. With right sides together, pin a sash to each side of one pieced strip, as shown in scaled piecing diagram (sashes were cut slightly long to allow for variations in piecing; trim off any excess). Be careful not to stretch pieces, but be sure they lie flat. Stitch ¼-inch seams, remove pins, and iron seams toward sashes.

4. With right sides together, and turning triangles in opposite direction to those in center strip, pin remaining pieced strips on outside edges of sashes, as shown in scaled piecing diagram. Be careful that triangles align across and that ends are even; you may have to ease some pieces gently to get a perfect match. Stitch ¼-inch seams, remove pins, and iron seams toward sashes. Then iron whole piece carefully with steam iron to be sure it is square and flat.

5. With right sides together, pin short end borders to ends of pieced rectangle. These were also cut long to allow for variations in piecing; trim off any excess (Illustration C). Stitch ¼-inch seams, remove pins, and iron seams toward borders.

6. In a similar manner, join side borders to sides of pieced rectangle. They were also cut long, so trim off any excess.

7. Working on a flat surface, lay pieced top on backing, wrong sides together. Keeping entire piece square, pin pieces together and baste by hand with long stitches about 1 inch from raw edges. Cut off excess backing. You may stabilize the two pieces by machine-stitching with a long stitch about ¼ inch from raw edges.

8. To make binding, refer to page 147. With right sides together, start pinning binding to one long edge of runner ⅜ inch from raw edges. Stitch ⅜-inch seam. Miter each corner by ending stitching ⅜ inch from upcoming corner, backstitch, and finish. Fold a small pleat into binding at corner, then start stitching again ⅜ inch along on next side. Continue in this manner all the way around quilt. Cut off excess binding, leaving a small overlap; turn raw edge under, and blind-stitch by hand. Finish binding on wrong side by hand, as described on page 147. Remove pins and basting. Iron binding gently to flatten.

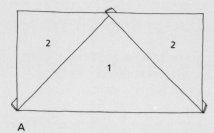

A

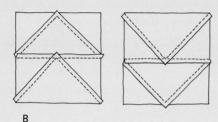

B

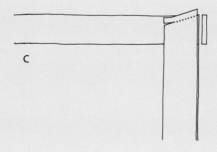

C

MATERIALS

- 1⅞ yards dark green cotton plaid for backing, binding, and borders
- 1⅞ yards dark green cotton print for sashes
- Approximately ½ yard total of dark cotton print scraps
- Approximately ½ yard total of light cotton print scraps
- 1 spool green or neutral thread

◆

CUT

- Green plaid backing piece, 66 x 22 inches (trim to exact size after joining to pieced front)
- 5 yards 2-inch-wide green plaid bias binding (see page 147)
- 2 green plaid borders, 17 x 2⅜ inches
- 2 green plaid borders, 66 x 2⅜ inches
- 2 green print sashes, 62 x 2⅜ inches
- 90 dark #1 triangles
- 180 light #2 triangles

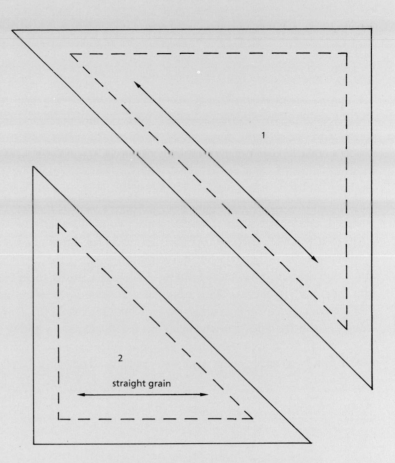

1

2

straight grain

All pattern pieces, and cutting guide for sashes and borders, are full size. Arrows indicate straight grain of fabric.

seam allowance

cutting guide for sashes and borders

AMISH STAR PILLOWS

Quilts made by the Amish are known for their intense, solid colors and eye-catching designs. Always simple, the designs are composed mainly of squares, triangles, and rectangles. The Star pattern that appears on the pillows at right was adapted from a pattern that frequently appears in Amish quilts.

Although the three pillows look quite different, each was pieced from the same pattern pieces. The variations were created by changing the colors of the triangles and squares: the middle pillow appears to have a larger center square because adjoin-ing pieces were cut from the same color. Using the same fabric but changing the grain line can also alter the visual effect, since the surfaces of the pieces will catch the light differently, as in the pillow at far left. If you make more than one pillow, you may want to experiment with different color combinations for the pieces.

Choose a sturdy plain-weave cotton or cotton-polyester blend that has an attractive surface finish. Fabrics with glazed or satiny surfaces work especially well. Hard-finish wools or silks can also be effective.

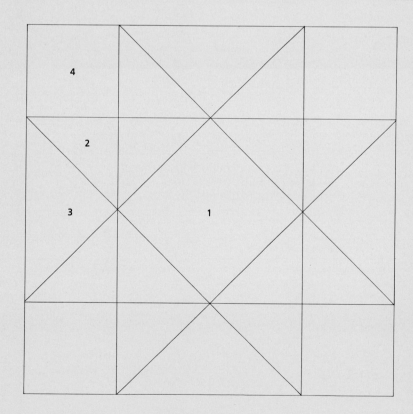

Scaled piecing diagram Shown here in reduction is the exact arrangement of the pieces in the pillows at right.

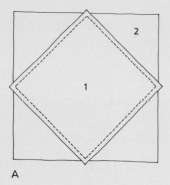

A

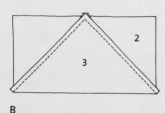

B

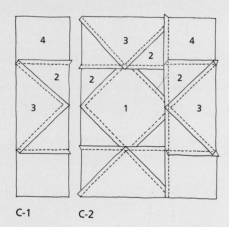

C-1   C-2

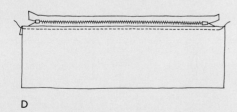

D

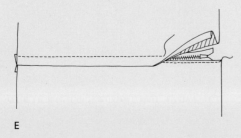

E

MATERIALS

(for each pillow)

- ½ yard main-color dress-weight cotton or cotton-polyester blend •
- ⅛ yard each of two contrasting colors, similar fabric •
- 12-inch lightweight zipper to match main color •
- 1 spool thread to match main color •
- 14-inch muslin pillow form, available in fabric or notions stores •

ASSEMBLY

Each of the finished pillows is 14 inches square. See the General Directions, pages 144-147, for suggested sewing equipment, notes on fabric, and instructions for making and using pattern templates, pinning and cutting fabric, piecing by hand or by machine, and making bias binding.

1. With right sides together, pin long edges of the four first-contrast-color #2 pieces to edges of #1 piece. Stitch ¼-inch seams, remove pins, and iron seams toward #2 pieces (Illustration A).

2. With right sides together, pin long edges of the eight second-contrast-color #2 pieces to short edges of #3 pieces. Stitch ¼-inch seams, remove pins, and iron seams toward #2 pieces (Illustration B).

3. With right sides together, pin one #4 piece to each end of two of the rectangles. Stitch ¼-inch seams, remove pins, and iron seams toward #4 pieces (Illustration C-1).

4. With right sides together, pin remaining two rectangles to opposite sides of center square assembly, carefully matching points of #1 and #3 pieces. Stitch ¼-inch seams, remove pins, and iron seams toward center square. Complete pillow top by pinning and stitching two side strips to long sides of center rectangle, carefully matching points of #1 and #3 pieces and corners of #2 and #4 pieces (Illustration C-2). Stitch ¼-inch seams, remove pins, and iron seams toward center square. Iron top carefully and set it aside.

5. To attach zipper to pillow back, begin by ironing under ½ inch along one long edge of narrower back piece. Place this folded edge down on zipper tape so that fold almost touches teeth and zipper ends are equidistant from each end of fabric (Illustration D). Pin zipper in place at each end. Hand-baste along fold if desired to secure zipper. Stitch close to folded edge of fabric. Remove pins.

6. Iron under ⅝ inch along one long edge of wider back piece. Lay this over zipper so that it just covers stitching on first piece. Pin in place, and baste if desired. When you put zipper foot down so that it clears ridge of zipper, you should be able to stitch ½ inch from folded edge of this overlapped piece, catching raw edge of turned fabric. Stitch into 1-inch area beyond each end of zipper (Illustration E). Remove pins.

7. With right sides together, lay pieced pillow top on pillow back, leaving zipper partly open. Extra ⅛-inch seam allowance on back will show beyond edges of top. Pin along ¼-inch seam allowance on pieced top and stitch all the way around. Remove pins, and clip corners.

8. Turn piece right side out through zipper opening. At corners, gently push out seams with wooden knitting needle or other blunt-tipped instrument to make them square up. Insert pillow form through zipper opening by folding or squeezing. Smooth cover over form and zip zipper.

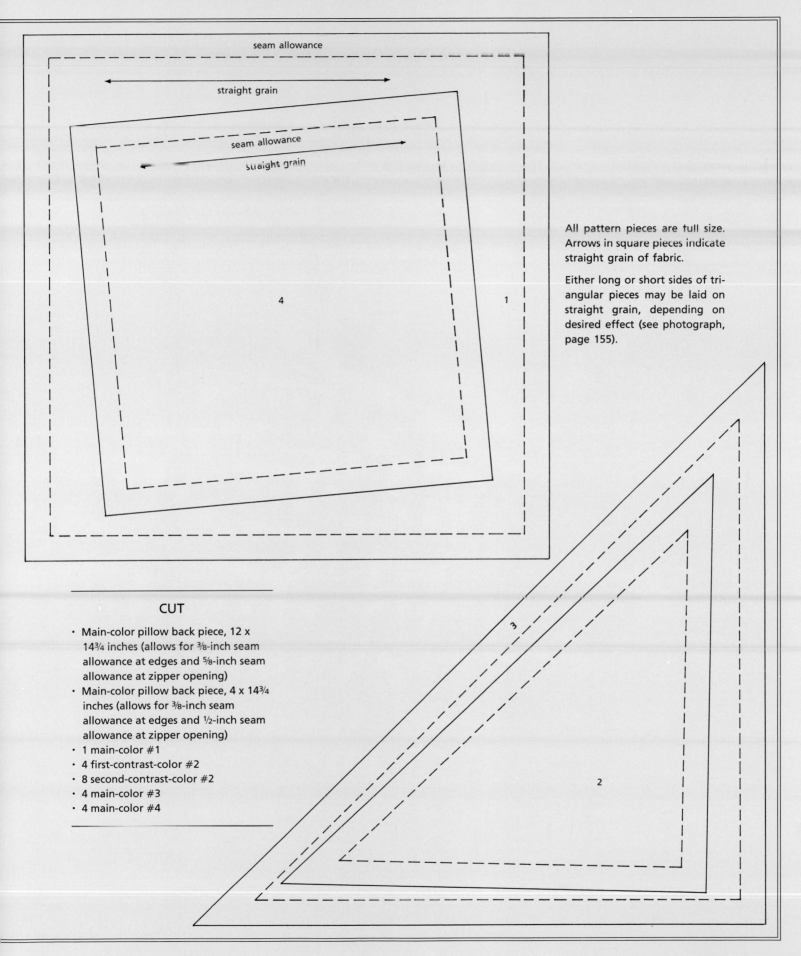

seam allowance

straight grain

seam allowance

straight grain

4

1

All pattern pieces are full size. Arrows in square pieces indicate straight grain of fabric.

Either long or short sides of triangular pieces may be laid on straight grain, depending on desired effect (see photograph, page 155).

3

2

CUT

- Main-color pillow back piece, 12 x 14¾ inches (allows for ⅜-inch seam allowance at edges and ⅝-inch seam allowance at zipper opening)
- Main-color pillow back piece, 4 x 14¾ inches (allows for ⅜-inch seam allowance at edges and ½-inch seam allowance at zipper opening)
- 1 main-color #1
- 4 first-contrast-color #2
- 8 second-contrast-color #2
- 4 main-color #3
- 4 main-color #4

LITTLE SCHOOLHOUSE QUILT

Possibly the most appealing of all youthful quilt designs is the Little Schoolhouse. It exists in many variations, and has been made for generations in every conceivable color combination and block size.

The very small quilt shown here comprises 5½-inch-square blocks bordered with sashes. It is not only ideal for a crib or cradle, but would make a good nursery wall hanging or a doll quilt for an older child.

Because the blocks have been designed to be pieced in segments using only straight seams, this quilt is easily sewn by machine, although it is also a good size for sewing by hand. As you can see from the scaled piecing diagram, the quilt is designed so that segments of the house intentionally don't match—and it has been sewn with deliberate unevenness—making it look more like the work of a child.

Such a small textile piece probably needs no batting, though it could certainly be added. If you decide to use batting, follow the instructions on pages 146-147. While the directions call for tying, you could also quilt a very simple design around the blocks and sashes.

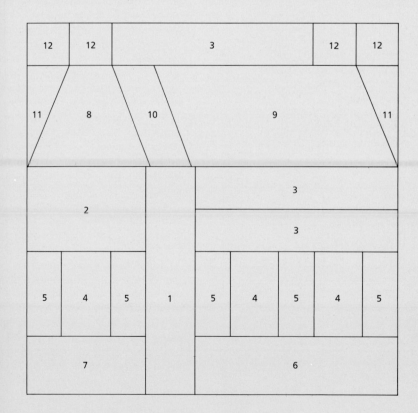

Scaled piecing diagram Shown here in reduction is the exact arrangement of the pieces in one block of the quilt at left.

MATERIALS

(to make the quilt in the colors shown here)

- ¾ yard unbleached muslin for backing and white pieces in schoolhouse blocks
- Approximately ⅜ yard total of various mini-print red cottons
- Approximately ⅜ yard total of various print or solid navy cottons
- 1 yard red #5 pearl cotton or other fine embroidery floss
- 1 spool neutral thread

CUT

(for each of 12 blocks)

- 1 white #1
- 2 white #3
- 3 white #4
- 1 white #10
- 1 white #11
- 3 white #11 reversed
- 2 white #12

- 1 red #2
- 1 red #3
- 5 red #5
- 1 red #6
- 1 red #7
- 1 red #8
- 1 red #9
- 2 red #12

(for remainder of quilt)

- 17 dark blue print sash pieces
- 6 light blue print corner blocks
- 2 plain navy framing strips, 1¼ x 27 inches for sides
- 2 plain navy framing strips, 1¼ x 21½ inches for top and bottom
- Muslin backing piece, 29 x 22 inches

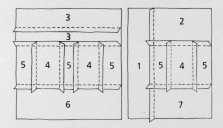

A

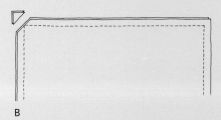

B

ASSEMBLY

The finished quilt is 28 x 21 inches. See the General Directions, pages 144-147, for suggested sewing equipment, notes on fabric, and instructions for making and using pattern templates, pinning and cutting fabric, and piecing by hand or by machine. It is suggested that you keep all the pieces for each block in separate plastic bags. It is also a good idea to cut and stitch the pieces for one block first, to make sure that you understand how to do it. Then proceed to cut and sew the remaining eleven blocks, sashes, and so on.

1. With right sides together, pin together a #5, #4, and #5 piece for left window section. Then pin a #5, #4, #5, #4, and #5 piece for right window section (see scaled piecing diagram). Stitch ¼-inch seams, remove pins, and iron seams toward #5 pieces.

2. In a similar manner, pin and stitch one red #3 and one white #3 together, ironing seam toward red piece. Make up right and left sides of schoolhouse by pinning and stitching red #3 piece and #6 piece to right window section, and pinning and stitching #2 and #7 pieces to left window section. Remove pins, and iron all seams toward red pieces. Pin and stitch right and left side sections to #1 piece. Remove pins, and iron seams toward #1 piece, as they will lie flatter that way (Illustration A).

3. As in Step 1, pin and stitch together remaining segments: roof and sky—a #8, #9, #10, and two #11—and chimneys and sky—a #3, two red #12, and two white #12. Remove pins, and iron seams toward darker pieces. Pin and stitch the three main sections—chimneys, roof, and windows—together following scaled piecing diagram. Remove pins, and iron seams toward roof section. Iron whole block so that it is square. Measure block; with seam allowances included, it should be 6 inches square.

4. As in Step 1, pin and stitch together three vertical strips, each composed of four schoolhouse blocks separated by three sash pieces. Then pin and stitch together two narrow vertical strips, each composed of four sash pieces separated by three corner blocks. Remove pins, and iron all seams in both sets of strips toward sashes.

5. With right sides together, pin schoolhouse block strips together alternately with corner block strips, as shown in photograph on page 158. Be sure that corners of horizontal sash strips and corner blocks match up exactly, without stretching or puckering, and that all strips come out the same length. Stitch ¼-inch seams, remove pins, and iron all seams toward narrow strips.

6. With right sides together, pin side framing strips to sides of pieced section. Stitch ¼-inch seams, remove pins, and iron seams toward framing strips. Join top and bottom framing strips in same way. Iron whole top carefully with steam iron to be sure it is square and flat.

7. Lay top face down on muslin back. Back was cut a little large, so pin top to back along ¼-inch seam allowance of top, leaving an opening of about 6 inches at one side. Stitch ¼-inch seam, then cut off excess back seam allowance. Cut off corners (Illustration B).

8. Turn quilt right side out through opening. At corners, gently push out seams with wooden knitting needle or other blunt-tipped instrument to make them square up. Iron edges flat. Pin opening together. With fine needle and thread, stitch opening closed as inconspicuously as possible. Iron edges so that they are sharp and even.

9. To tie quilt on back, pin through layers at several points so that back and front lie smoothly together. With large needle and embroidery thread, take a stitch up through center of each block and another stitch down about ¼ inch away. Tie thread on back, and cut ends.

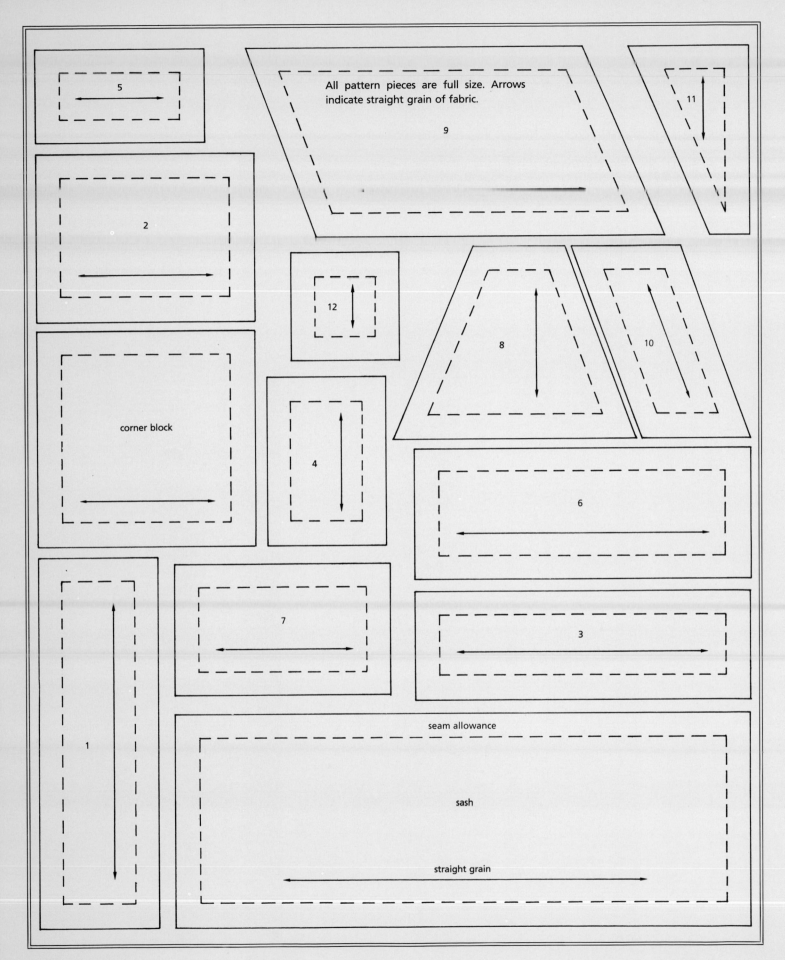

VASE OF TULIPS QUILT

The Vase of Tulips pattern used on the block-appliqué quilt shown here was adapted from an original design by Ann Orr, a well-known 20th-century quilt designer. This pattern is often made in the pastels favored in the 1930s, but small floral prints would also work well.

A standard square quilt of this size—composed of sixteen 14-inch-square blocks, separated by sashes—fits a twin or double bed; it can also be used as a coverlet over a plain bedspread on a queen-size bed. To increase the size, simply add another tier of blocks or widen the borders.

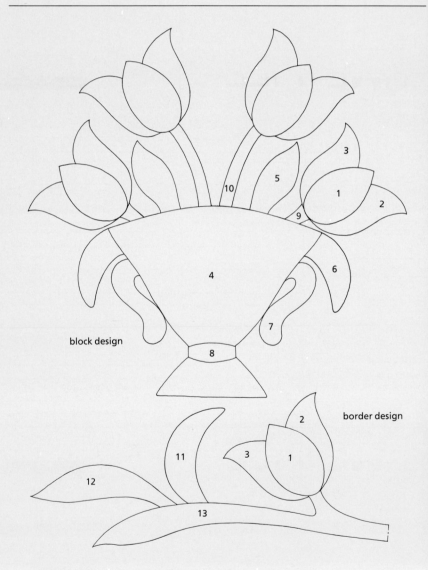

block design

border design

Scaled appliqué diagram Shown here in reduction are the exact arrangements of the pieces in one block and border section of the quilt at right.

162

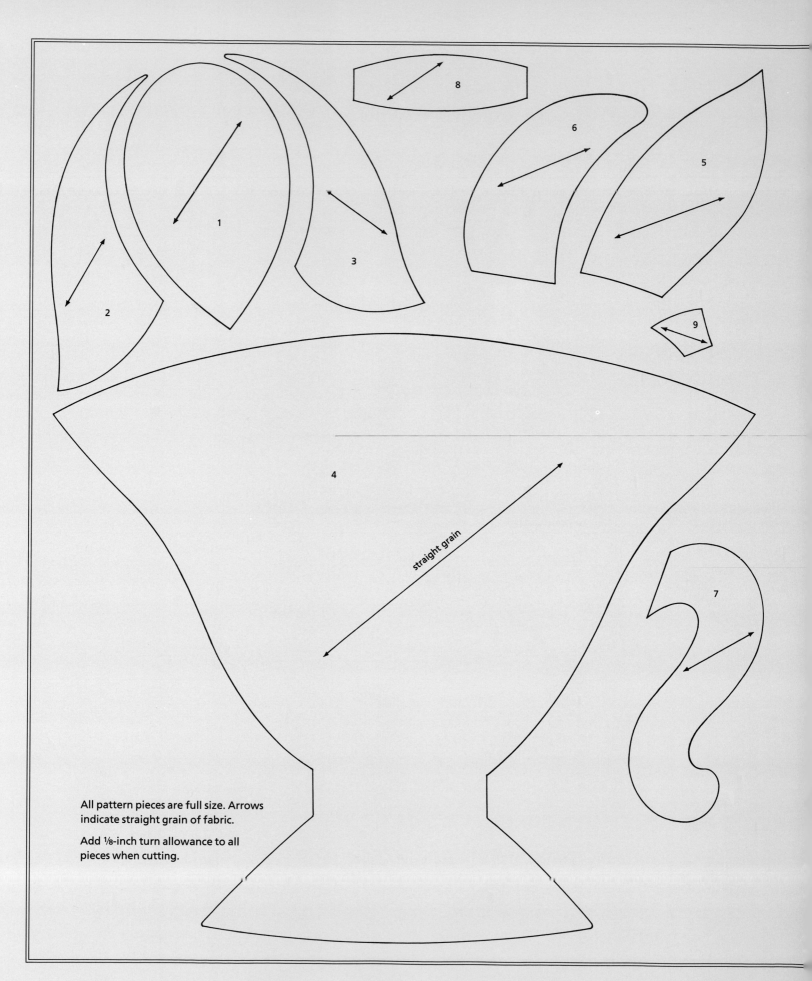

All pattern pieces are full size. Arrows indicate straight grain of fabric.

Add ⅛-inch turn allowance to all pieces when cutting.

straight grain

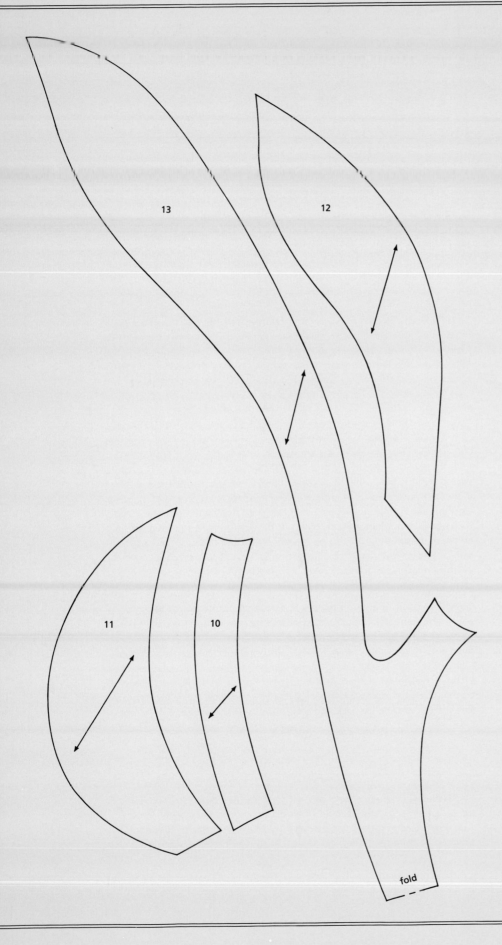

MATERIALS

(To make the quilt in the colors shown here; yardages are based on 45-inch-wide fabric.)

- 5½ yards soft white fabric for quilt top
- 5 yards same or contrasting fabric for backing
- ¾ yard royal blue for vases
- 1¾ yards soft green for stems, leaves, and bias binding
- ½ yard each of two shades of yellow, pink, and lavender for flowers
- ⅜ yard black or navy for trim on vases
- 1 double bed quilt batt
- 4 large spools white sewing thread
- Threads to match colors or 2 spools neutral thread for appliqué

◆

CUT

(A ¼-inch seam allowance is included in the measurement of each piece.)

- 16 white squares, 14½ x 14½ inches
- 12 white short sashes, 14½ x 3½ inches
- 3 white long sashes, 65½ x 3½ inches
- 2 white end borders, 65½ x 7¼ inches
- 2 white side borders, 79 x 7¼ inches
- 9 yards 2-inch-wide green bias binding (see page 147)

(for each of 16 blocks)

- 4 pastel #1 (in choice of colors)
- 4 pastel #2 (in choice of colors)
- 4 pastel #3 (in same colors as #2)
- 1 royal blue #4
- 1 green #5 and 1 green #5 reversed
- 1 green #6 and 1 green #6 reversed
- 1 black #7 and 1 black #7 reversed
- 1 black #8
- 1 green #9 and 1 green #9 reversed
- 1 green #10 and 1 green #10 reversed

(for each of 10 border motifs)

- 2 pastel #1 (in choice of colors)
- 2 pastel #2 (in choice of colors)
- 2 pastel #3 (in same colors as #2)
- 1 green #11 and 1 green #11 reversed
- 1 green #12 and 1 green #12 reversed
- 1 green #13 (place on fold)

DIRECTIONS

The finished quilt is 79 inches square. See the General Directions, pages 144-147, for suggested sewing equipment, notes on fabric, and instructions for making and using pattern templates, pinning and cutting fabric, backing, filling, and quilting the finished top, and making bias binding.

APPLIQUE

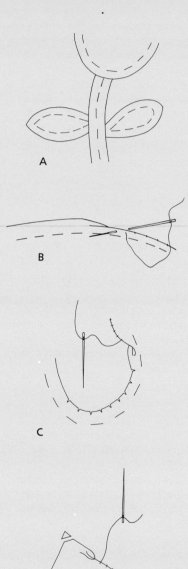

So that all the blocks look identical, make a full-size drawing of the scaled appliqué diagram; then with a sharp pencil, trace the drawing onto each fabric square using a light-box or holding the fabric against a window. It is also permissible to work by eye from the diagram, since slight variations in the blocks can lend the quilt a certain charm. In general, the turn allowance for appliqué pieces is about ⅛ inch—slightly more for loosely woven or heavy fabric.

1. Pin each piece in place on block or border according to scaled appliqué diagram or your tracing. Baste each piece to block slightly more than ¼ inch from edge to prevent having to baste through two appliqué pieces at once (Illustration A). Remove pins. When sewing pieces to block, layer them according to appliqué diagram as follows: #2, #3, #9, and #10 pieces will have #1 piece stitched over them; #4 piece covers edges of all other pieces except #8.

2. To turn under edges you are to appliqué, use your fingers or the point of your needle. If basting is correctly placed, just over ¼ inch from edge, you will only be able to turn under allotted ⅛ inch.

3. To appliqué invisibly, use a neutral thread, or match thread color to each piece. The best stitch to use is the blind stitch, worked in the following manner: Knot one end of thread. Bring needle up through block fabric, catching just a few threads of folded edge of appliqué piece. Put needle back down through base fabric only, just beyond folded edge from where it emerged. In same motion, bring needle up farther along folded edge exactly as you did for first stitch (Illustration B). At first your stitches may be as much as ¼ inch apart, but as you gain expertise they should be ⅛ inch or less apart, and evenly spaced.

Note: Two difficult areas in sewing appliqué are inside, or concave, curves and sharp points. Making the stitches smaller makes concave curves easier to do, but it is often necessary, using a very fine, sharp scissors, to make short cuts—barely more than 1/16 inch—into the turn allowance perpendicular to the edge (Illustration C). For sharp points, such as those at the ends of the leaves, a small triangle should be trimmed from the ends (Illustration D); be sure not to cut as deeply as the turn line. Take several extra tiny stitches around the point to secure the turn allowance.

ASSEMBLY

1. When all sixteen blocks and all four borders have been completely appliquéd, iron them and hang them over a rack to keep them smooth.

2. Pin together four long vertical strips, each composed of four appliqué blocks separated by three short sashes, as shown in overall diagram. Stitch sashes and blocks together, leaving ¼-inch seams. Remove pins, and iron seams toward sashes (Illustration E).

3. Pin a long sash between each of these four strips, as shown in overall diagram. Stitch sashes and strips together, leaving ¼-inch seam allowances. Be very careful that when pieces are joined, short sashes run in straight line, broken only by long sashes. If you have not measured sizes of blocks and sashes carefully when making up strips, you may have to rip out and resew some seams. It is worth taking extra time to have entire top look neat and square. Remove pins, and iron seams toward sashes. When block assembly is completed, all blocks should be exactly 14 inches square, and all sashes should be exactly 3 inches wide.

4. In similar manner, pin and stitch top and bottom borders to ends of block assembly. Remove pins, and iron seams toward borders. Pin and stitch side borders to sides of block assembly and end borders. Remove pins, and iron seams toward borders. Top is now complete.

5. To assemble quilt layers, follow instructions for batting, backing, and quilting on pages 146-147, and in Quilting Frames, pages 148-149.

6. To quilt, you may use a solid diagonal line or crosshatch, coupled with one line of quilting around appliqué pieces, adding any small motifs you wish in block corners, and continuous designs in sashes.

7. When quilting is completed and top has been removed from frame, trim edges evenly. Trim corners into gentle curves, to make binding easier. Baste all layers together about ¼ inch from raw edge of top.

8. To make bias binding, refer to page 147. With right sides together, start pinning binding to one long side of quilt ⅜ inch from raw edges, and continue all around, easing binding around corner curves. Stitch ⅜-inch seam. Cut off end of binding, leaving small overlap to be folded under, covering raw end where binding began. Finish on wrong side by hand as described in General Directions. Press edges gently to flatten bias binding.

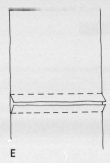

E

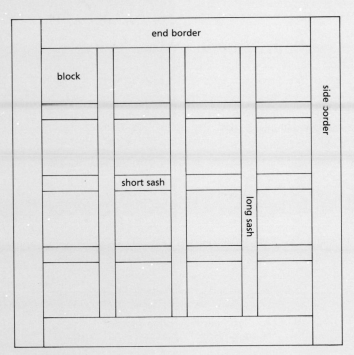

Overall diagram

Selected Reading

Bacon, Lenice Ingram. *American Patchwork Quilts*. New York: William Morrow & Company, 1973.

Binney, Edwin, 3rd, and Gail Binney-Winslow. *Homage to Amanda: Two Hundred Years of American Quilts*. San Francisco: R K Press, 1984.

Bishop, Robert, and Carter Houck. *All Flags Flying*. New York: E.P. Dutton, 1986.

Bishop, Robert, and Patricia Coblentz. *New Discoveries in American Quilts*. New York: E.P. Dutton, 1975.

Brooks, Vicki, and Linda Stokes. *The Quilter's Catalog: A Complete Guide to Quilting Sources and Supplies*. Pittstown, N.J.: The Main Street Press, 1987.

Bullard, Lacy Folmar, and Betty Jo Shiell. *Chintz Quilts: Unfading Glory*. Tallahassee, Fla.: Serendipity Publishers, 1983.

Duke, Dennis, and Deborah Harding, eds. *America's Glorious Quilts*. New York: Hugh Lauter Levin Associates, 1987.

Ferrero, Pat, Elaine Hedges, and Julie Silber. *Hearts and Hands: The Influence of Women & Quilts on American Society*. San Francisco: The Quilt Digest Press, 1987.

Florence, Cathy Gaines. *Collecting Quilts: Investments in America's Heritage*. Paducah, Ky.: American Quilter's Society, 1985.

Green, Caroline. *Quilting*. Mississauga, Ont.: Cupress, 1987.

Gwinner, Schnuppe von. *The History of the Patchwork Quilt: Origins, Traditions and Symbols of a textile art*. West Chester, Pa.: Schiffer Publishing, 1988.

Holstein, Jonathan. *The Pieced Quilt: An American Design Tradition*. Greenwich, Conn.: New York Graphic Society, 1973.

James, Michael. *The Quiltmaker's Handbook: A Guide to Design and Construction*. Englewood Cliffs, N.J.: Prentice-Hall, 1978.

Khin, Yvonne M. *The Collector's Dictionary of Quilt Names & Patterns*. Washington, D.C.: Acropolis Books, 1985.

Kolter, Jane Bentley. *Forget Me Not: A Gallery of Friendship and Album Quilts*. Pittstown, N.J.: The Main Street Press, 1985.

Lasansky, Jeannette. *Pieced By Mother: Over 100 Years Of Quiltmaking Traditions*. Lewisburg, Pa.: Oral Traditions Project of the Union County Historical Society, 1987.

Lipsett, Linda Otto. *Remember Me: Women & Their Friendship Quilts*. San Francisco: The Quilt Digest Press, 1985.

Marston, Gwen, and Joe Cunningham. *Amish Quilting Patterns: 56 Full-Size Ready-to-Use Designs and Complete Instructions*. New York: Dover Publications, 1987.

McMorris, Penny. *Crazy Quilts*. New York: E.P. Dutton, 1984.

Nelson, Cyril I., and Carter Houck. *Treasury of American Quilts: Including complete patterns and instructions for making your own quilts*. New York: Greenwich House, 1984.

Orlofsky, Patsy and Myron. *Quilts in America*. New York: McGraw-Hill Book Company, 1974.

Pellman, Rachel and Kenneth. *Amish Doll Quilts, Dolls, and Other Playthings*. Intercourse, Pa.: Good Books, 1986.

Pellman, Rachel and Kenneth. *The World of Amish Quilts*. Intercourse, Pa.: Good Books, 1984.

Safford, Carleton L., and Robert Bishop. *America's Quilts and Coverlets*. New York: E.P. Dutton, 1972.

The Quilt Digest Press. *The Quilt Digest*, vol. 1 (and subsequent annual volumes). San Francisco: The Quilt Digest Press, 1983.

Walker, Michele. *The Complete Book of Quiltmaking*. New York: Alfred A. Knopf, 1986.

Woodard, Thos. K., and Blanche Greenstein. *Classic American Quilts*. New York: Portland House, 1987.

Woodard, Thos. K., and Blanche Greenstein. *Crib Quilts and Other Small Wonders: Including complete patterns and instructions for making your own crib quilts*. New York: E.P. Dutton, 1981.

Photography and Illustration Credits

Cover and pages 100-101, 118-119, 124-125, 130, 142, 155: Stephen Donelian. Frontispiece and pages 110, 112, 114-117, 123, 126, 136-137, 163: George Ross. Pages 8, 20, 28, 41, 42, 56 (top), 66-67, 108: Myron Miller. Pages 10, 12, 13, 15, 16, 22, 25, 29, 30, 31, 32, 33, 34, 36, 37, 40, 44, 49, 50, 56 (top), 58, 60-61, 68, 72, 74, 75, 80-81, 83, 84, 86, 91, 92 (except top), 93, 94, 102, 105 (bottom): America Hurrah, NYC. Pages 11, 18, 19, 92 (top): Shelburne Museum, Shelburne, VT. Pages 14, 26, 27, 39, 90, 103, 105 (top): Oral Traditions Project of the Union County Historical Society, Lewisburg, PA. Pages 17, 62, 65 (top left), 85, 99: from the collection of The Kentucky Historical Society, Frankfort, KY. Pages 21, 23 (courtesy Eve Wilson), 24, 35, 38, 43, 45, 48, 53, 59 (right), 70, 73, 82, 105 (center), 106: Thos. K. Woodard/American Antiques & Quilts, NYC. Pages 46, 47, 96, 97, 107: Robert Bishop. Page 52: courtesy of Hirschl & Adler Folk, NYC. Page 54: Ray Featherstone, The Country Shop, Westfield, IN. Page 55: Jay Johnson/America's Folk Heritage Gallery, NYC. Pages 59 (left), 63: Museum of American Folk Art, NYC. Pages 64-65 (top row, left to right): Terry Ackerman and Pat Yamin; Oregon Historical Society, Portland, OR (negative number 21876); The Kentucky Historical Society, Frankfort, KY; Pat Yamin/Come Quilt With Me, Brooklyn, NY; (bottom row, left to right): Culver Pictures, NYC; Bettmann Archive, NYC; Bettmann Archive; Culver Pictures; Culver Pictures. Pages 69, 71: Museum of Fine Arts, Boston. Page 76: Honolulu Academy of Arts, Honolulu, HI. Page 77: quilt made by Eleanor Anderson, courtesy of Honolulu Academy of Arts, Honolulu, HI. Pages 88-89, 134, 135: David Phelps. Pages 87, 95, 98, 109, 148-149, 158: Alan Shortall. Page 104: Valentine Museum, Richmond, VA. Pages 113, 120-122, 127-129, 132-133, 139, 140, 150-151: Jon Elliott. Pages 131, 144-147, 151-154, 156-157, 159-162, 164-167: illustrations by William J. Meyerriecks. Pages 138, 141: Bradley Olman.

Prop Credits

The Editors would like to thank the following for their courtesy in lending items for photography. Items not listed below are privately owned. **Cover**: Amish quilt and blue-and-white quilt—Thos. K. Woodard, American Antiques & Quilts, NYC; signature quilt—Ilisha Helfman and Joe Freedman. **Page 56**: Top photo: quilt made by Alice Hegy and Arnold Savage. Bottom photo: quilt created by the parents and teachers of The Day School, NYC. **Page 57**: Top photo: quilt from the collection of the Flushing Area Historical Society, Flushing, MI, made by Caron L. Mosey. Bottom photo: quilt designed by Erwin Rowland of Erwin Rowland Quilts & Counterpanes, NYC. **Page 87**: all quilts—Judith and James Milne/American Country Antiques, NYC. **Pages 88-89**: antique white quilt—Laura Fisher/Antique Quilts and Americana, NYC; antique wooden templates—Berdan's Antiques, Hallowell, ME; tin templates—Lorin Tuttle, Eastport, NY, and Elaine Wilmarth, Glen Dale, MD; cardboard, cereal box, and paper templates—Pat Yamin/Come Quilt With Me, Brooklyn, NY; Barbara Brackman, Lawrence, KS; Needleart Guild, Grand Rapids, MI. **Pages 100-101**: fabrics—The Watermelon Patch, Manhasset, NY; pine table—Pine Country Antiques, NYC. **Page 109**: all quilts—Judith and James Milne/American Country Antiques, NYC. **Page 110**: stenciling by Lynn Goodpasture, NYC; Honeycomb quilt—Susan Parrish Antiques, NYC; Star quilt—Cynthia Beneduce Antiques, NYC. **Page 112**: quilts—Jeannine Dobbs Antiques, Merrimack, NH. **Pages 114-115**: quilt designed and made by Karen Berkenfeld, NYC. **Pages 118-119**: storage instructions courtesy of The Textile Conservation Workshop, South Salem, NY; acid-free boxes and tissue paper—Talas, NYC; quilts—Judith and James Milne/American Country Antiques, NYC. **Pages 120-121**: antiques and interiors—June Worrell Antiques, Houston, TX. **Page 122**: interior designed by June Worrell Antiques, Houston, TX. **Pages 124-125**: antique crib and doll quilts courtesy of: Bettie Mintz, Bethesda, MD; Laura Fisher/Antique Quilts and Americana, NYC; Judith and James Milne/American Country Antiques, NYC; Victoria Hoffman, NYC; quilt racks—Alice Bennett/Primrose Lane, Manhasset, NY; antique doll bed—Laura Fisher/Antique Quilts and Americana. **Page 127**: antiques and interiors—June Worrell Antiques, Houston, TX. **Pages 130-131**: consultant—Tracey Jamar/Jamar Textile Restoration Studio, NYC. **Page 133**: antiques and interiors—June Worrell Antiques, Houston, TX. **Pages 134-135**: antiques shop and quilts—Larry Zingale and Marge King/Warwick Valley Antiques, NY. **Pages 136-137**: designed by Renée Leonard, NYC; antiques and accessories—Eggs & Tricity, NYC. **Page 138**: designed by Riki Gail Interiors, NYC. **Page 140**: antiques and interiors—June Worrell Antiques, Houston, TX. **Page 141**: designed by Riki Gail Interiors, NYC. **Page 142**: square pincushions, small spool holder, small scissors—Alice Bennett/Primrose Lane, Manhasset, NY; tape measure and selected fabrics—The Watermelon Patch, Manhasset, NY; all other quilting supplies—Pat Yamin/Come Quilt With Me,

Brooklyn, NY. **Pages 148-149**: ratchet frame—People's Place, Intercourse, PA; ladder-back chairs—Shaker Workshops, Concord, MA; hoop frame—Pat Yamin/Come Quilt With Me, Brooklyn, NY; Schoolhouse quilt and Basket quilt—made by Linda Mason of The Watermelon Patch, Manhasset, NY; Sunshine and Shadow variation quilt—made by Polly Whitehorn, Great Neck, NY. **Page 150**: antiques and interiors—June Worrell Antiques, Houston, TX; table runner—made by Linda Mason of The Watermelon Patch, Manhasset, NY. **Pages 154-155**: pillows—made by Linda Mason of The Watermelon Patch, Manhasset, NY. **Pages 158-159**: Little Schoolhouse crib quilt cow pull toy, and painted toy chest—The Watermelon Patch, Manhasset, NY; braided rug—ABC International Design Rugs, NYC; crib, antique lace pillows, and linens—Alice Bennett/Primrose Lane, Manhasset, NY; fabric teddy bear—ABC Linens, NYC; hand-woven baby blanket—Treadles, NYC. **Pages 162-163**: Vase of Tulips quilt—James Alessio, Ole Kentucky Quilts, Woodbury, CT.

Index